BEITRÄGE ZUR
GESCHICHTE DER BIBLISCHEN EXEGESE

Herausgegeben von

OSCAR CULLMANN, BASEL/PARIS · NILS A. DAHL, NEW HAVEN
ERNST KÄSEMANN, TÜBINGEN · HANS-JOACHIM KRAUS, GÖTTINGEN
HEIKO A. OBERMAN, TÜBINGEN · HARALD RIESENFELD, UPSALA
KARL HERMANN SCHELKLE, TÜBINGEN

19

A History of Interpretation of Hebrews 7,1-10 from the Reformation to the Present

by

BRUCE DEMAREST

1 9 7 6

J. C. B. MOHR (PAUL SIEBECK) TÜBINGEN

CIP-Kurztitelaufnahme der Deutschen Bibliothek

Demarest, Bruce
A history of interpretation of Hebrews 7, 1—10 [seven one to ten]
from the reformation to the present. — 1. Aufl. — Tübingen: Mohr, 1976.
(Beiträge zur Geschichte der biblischen Exegese; 19)
ISBN 3-16-138531-4
ISSN 0408-8298

Revision of A Thesis
for the Degree Doctor of Philosophy
at the University of Manchester, England

FORWARD

The present study represents an adaptation of a thesis
presented in October 1973 to the University of Manchester
(England) in support of the degree of Doctor of Philosophy.
The original project was more extensive in scope in that it
traced the interpretation, from the Reformation to the present, of the seventh chapter of Hebrews in its entirety. With
a view to publication in the present series the writer adopted
the recommendation of the editors by limiting the study to
a consideration of the history of interpretation of the Melchizedek motif in Hebrews 7:1-10. By thus reducing the bounds
of the study a lengthy manuscript was reduced to more readable
proportions while permitting interaction with several additional interpreters of this rich and profound New Testament
document.

The reader may judge that here and there a significant
interpreter of the Epistle has not been cited in the history.
Since no New Testament epistle has been more extensively com-
mentated upon than Hebrews, judicious selectivity of material
became imperative. If on occasion a significant interpreter
of Hebrews has been omitted in the history the lacuna may
be attributed to the absence of particularly distinctive
features in his exegesis. Diversity and breadth of opinion
are indispensable to a history of interpretation of a biblical text.

Gratitude must be expressed first of all to Professor F.
F. Bruce, Rylands Professor of Biblical Criticism and Exegesis in the University of Manchester, for his faithful guidance and encouragement throughout the course of the original
research. Professor Oscar Cullmann is likewise to be thanked
for his constructive suggestions with respect to both the
initial project and the present revision. Finally, gratitude
is due to the editorial committee for their guidance and to
the publisher, J. C. B. Mohr (Paul Siebeck), for the cour-
teous and efficient manner with which the manuscript was
processed.

Bruce A. Demarest

Denver, Colorado, U.S.A.
February, 1976

TABLE OF CONTENTS

LIST OF ABBREVIATIONS

Reference Works and Series

ADB   *Allgemeine Deutsche Biographie* (56 vols.; Leipzig, 1875-1912)

AG   Walter Bauer's, *A Greek-English Lexicon of the New Testament and Other Early Christian Literature*, trans. and adopted by W. F. Arndt and F. W. Gingrich (Chicago, 1957)

CGTSC   Cambridge Greek Testament for Schools and Colleges

CR   *Corpus Reformatorum* (87 vols.; Brunsviga, 1860-1900)

DNB   *Dictionary of National Biography* (63 vols.; London, 1885-1900)

EB   *Encyclopedia Britannica* (25 vols.; 9th. ed.; Edinburgh, 1875-89. 29 vols.; 11th. ed.; Cambridge, 1910-11)

EBib   Études Bibliques (Paris)

EGT   *Expositor's Greek Testament*, ed. by W. R. Nicoll

EJ   *Encyclopaedia Judaica* (16 vols.; Jerusalem, 1971)

HCNT   *Hand-Commentar zum Neuen Testament*, ed. by H. J. Holtzmann, etc.

HNT   Handbuch zum Neuen Testament, ed. by H. Leitzmann

ICC   The International Critical Commentary

ITL   International Theological Library

LSJ   *A Greek-English Lexicon*, by H. G. Liddell and R. Scott, rev. by H. S. Jones (Oxford, 1958)

MK   Kritisch-exegetischer Kommentar über das Neue Testament, begründet von H. A. W. Meyer

NCE   *The New Catholic Encyclopedia* (15 vols.; New York, 1967)

NIC   The New International Commentary on the New Testament, ed. by F. F. Bruce

SB   *Kommentar zum Neuen Testament aus Talmud und Midrasch*, by H. L. Strack and P. Billerbeck (4 vols.; München, 1922-28)

TU   *Texte und Untersuchungen zur Geschichte der altchristlichen Literatur* (Leipzig)

TWNT   *Theologisches Wörterbuch zum Neuen Testament*, ed. by G. Kittel and G. Friedrich (Stuttgart, 1931-). Vols. I-VIII are quoted in the ET: *Theological Dictionary of the New Testament*, trans. and ed. by G. Bromiley (Grand Rapids, 1964-)

WA   *D. Martin Luthers Werke*, kritische Gesamtausgabe (57 vols.; Weimar, 1883 ff.)

ZK   Kommentar zum Neuen Testament, ed. by T. Zahn

Journals

AJT	*American Journal of Theology* (Chicago)
Bib	*Biblica* (Rome)
CBQ	*Catholic Biblical Quarterly* (Washington, D. C.)
CJT	*Canadian Journal of Theology* (Toronto)
ExpT	*Expository Times* (Edinburgh)
IEJ.	*Israel Exploration Journal* (Jerusalem)
JBL	*Journal of Biblical Literature* (Philadelphia)
JTS	*Journal of Theological Studies* (Oxford)
NovT	*Novum Testamentum* (Leiden)
NTS	*New Testament Studies* (Cambridge)
PThR	*Princeton Theological Review* (Princeton, N.J.)
RB	*Revue Biblique* (Jerusalem)
RQ	*Revue de Qumran* (Paris)
SJT	*Scottish Journal of Theology* (Edinburgh)
ThLZ	*Theologische Literaturzeitung* (Leipzig)
ThSK	*Theologische Studien und Kritiken* (Hamburg, Gotha)
VetT	*Vetus Testamentum* (Leiden)
ZNW	*Zeitschrift für die neutestamentliche Wissenschaft* (Berlin)

I. INTRODUCTION

The worth of a history of interpretation of a biblical text is at least twofold. Initially, an inquiry into the manner in which a text has been understood and interpreted by the church through a period of its history ought to assist the student of the text to arrive at an exegesis as enlightened and responsible as possible. History bears witness to the fact that exegetical results examined and discarded by a consensus of responsible scholars in a former era are not infrequently returned to currency by interpreters uninitiated into the hard-fought exegetical conclusions of the past. Furnished with a survey of the interpretation of a text in history, the interpreter has at his command a valuable tool for attaining a right understanding of its meaning. A second rationale is that such a study uniquely mirrors the thought of the various historical periods considered.[1] Dogmatic assumptions and interpretive principles adopted by a particular movement or 'school' in a given era are held up to the light and examined for their true worth.[2] The reader is thereby enabled to grasp the causal relationship between dogmatic and hermeneutical presuppositions and the resultant exegesis. A useful dividend of an historical survey of this sort is often a refining of the principles of hermeneutics--in many cases how biblical exegesis ought not to be carried out.

An investigation of the history of interpretation of Heb 7:1-10 is a valuable undertaking. Unique amongst the writings of the NT the so-called 'epistle' to the Hebrews systematically develops as its central motif the theme of Christ as

---

1) See Kurt Aland, "Luther as an Exegete," ExpT, 69 (1957), 45, who cites this as a principal reason for scholarly interest in the history of exegesis of biblical texts.

2) An objective assessment of a movement or 'school' of interpretation can be made only in retrospect. Thus Karl Bornhauser comments concerning the difficulty of correctly evaluating one's immediate situation: "No theologian can write concerning the present without considering himself as part of that present, and without permitting his own participation in the movements to influence him." "The Present Status of Liberal Theology in Germany," AJT, 18 (1914), 191.

high priest.[1] The church has formulated its doctrine of the high priesthood of Christ principally from the teaching of this document. Chapter 7 of Hebrews constitutes the kernel and focus of the entire Epistle, since here the author develops in detail the enigmatic concept of priesthood "after the order of Melchizedek," a theological theme found nowhere else in the NT. Before explicating Jesus' radically new priestly order the writer must first unfold the significance of Melchizedek, the ancient priestly model who long ago foreshadowed the person and priesthood of Christ. A correct estimate of Christ's Melchizedekian priesthood (ch. 7:11-28) thus depends upon a correct interpretation of the writer's argument vis-à-vis Melchizedek (ch. 7:1-10). Apart from the major doctrinal significance of our text, the author advances a further rationale for the study at hand. The notion of the priesthood of Jesus "after the order of Melchizedek" is a λόγος δυσερμήνευτος[2]--a concept profound and mysterious, an idea difficult of explanation for any but the most enlightened.[3] The conceptions embodied in this radically new priestly order are denoted as ἡ στερεὰ τροφή for those that are τέλειος[4]--the most profound doctrines of the Christian religion.[5] In the third place, the enigmatic character of Melchizedek and the identification of Christ as a priest after his order have greatly stimulated the imagination of many who have undertaken to interpret this text. Consequently a wide range of opinion has been brought forward in respect

---

1) Whereas the Christological titles ἱερεύς and ἀρχιερεύς are found only in Hebrews, the idea of the priesthood of Jesus is implicit, at least, elsewhere in the NT. See Olaf Moe, "Das Priesterthum Christi im NT ausserhalb des Hebräerbriefes," *ThLZ*, 72 (1947), 335 ff. for a presentation of the evidence.

2) Heb 5:11.

3) "To one of the most difficult passages of the NT, to one of the old *cruces interpretum* belong the statements about Melchizedek in the seventh chapter of Hebrews." Karl August Auberlen, "Melchisedek's ewiges Leben und Priesterthum: Hebr 7," *ThSK*, 30 (1857), 453. Cf. also the comment of C.F.D. Moule: "The Epistle to the Hebrews has acquired a reputation for being formidable and remote from the world in which we live, and is consequently left severely alone even by some who try to read their Bibles seriously. How can . . . the shadowy figure of Melchizedek have anything to say to twentieth century faith?" "Commentaries on the Epistle to the Hebrews," *Theology*, 61 (1958), 228.

4) Heb 5:14.

5) Heb 6:1.

of it.[1] Thus the Christological significance of the text, its acknowledged difficulty, and the variety of interpretations which it has inspired provide sufficient rationale for undertaking a history of its exegesis.[2]

---

1) As far back as the seventeenth century John Owen could affirm: "There are almost as many different analyses given of this chapter as there are commentators upon it. And sometimes the same person proposeth sundry of them, without a determination of what he principally adheres unto." *Exercitations on the Epistle to the Hebrews* (4 vols.; London, 1668-74), III, 89.

2) A considerable corpus of literature has been stimulated by the biblical figure of Melchizedek, the most significant of which are mentioned. Gustave Bardy has surveyed Melchizedek speculation in Philo, the rabbis and the church fathers: "Melchisédech dans la tradition patristique," *RB*, 35 (1926), 496-509; 36 (1927), 25-45. Gottfried Wuttke, in a monograph entitled *Melchisedek der Priesterkönig von Salem* (Giessen, 1927), presents a survey of opinion in respect of Melchizedek through the patristic era. The dissertation prepared by F.J. Jérôme, *Das geschichtliche Melchisedek-Bild und seine Bedeutung im Hebräerbrief* (Freiburg, i.B., 1920), offers an interpretation of Heb 7:1-4 in the light of Gnostic sources, and an historical survey of the figure of Melchizedek in Jewish and Christian circles. However, Jérôme's survey of post-Reformation interpretation of the Melchizedek *Bild* in Gen 14: 18 ff., Psa 110:4 and Heb 7:1-4 is brief and sketchy. In the forward to his work Wuttke faults Jérôme for merely accumulating random excerpts from the history without an overall plan. Finally, mention should be made of the work of Helmuth Stork, *Die sogenannten Melchisedekianer* (Leipzig, 1928), which investigates the theological formulations of the heretical interpreters of the Melchizedek *Bild* between the second and fifth centuries and their refutation by early Christian apologists.

II. TEXT

1. Οὗτος γὰρ ὁ Μελχισέδεκ, βασιλεὺς Σαλήμ, ἱερεὺς τοῦ
θεοῦ τοῦ ὑψίστου, ὁ συναντήσας ᾿Αβραὰμ ὑποστρέφοντι ἀπὸ τῆς
κοπῆς τῶν βασιλέων καὶ εὐλογήσας αὐτόν, 2. ᾧ καὶ δεκάτην
ἀπὸ πάντων ἐμέρισεν ᾿Αβραάμ, πρῶτον μὲν ἑρμηνευόμενος βασιλεὺς
δικαιοσύνης ἔπειτα δὲ καὶ βασιλεὺς Σαλήμ, ὅ ἐστιν βασιλεὺς
εἰρήνης, 3. ἀπάτωρ, ἀμήτωρ, ἀγενεαλόγητος, μήτε ἀρχὴν ἡμερῶν
μήτε ζωῆς τέλος ἔχων, ἀφωμοιωμένος δὲ τῷ υἱῷ τοῦ θεοῦ, μένει
ἱερεὺς εἰς τὸ διηνεκές.

4. θεωρεῖτε δὲ πηλίκος οὗτος ᾧ δεκάτην ᾿Αβραὰμ ἔδωκεν ἐκ
τῶν ἀκροθινίων ὁ πατριάρχης. 5. καὶ οἱ μὲν ἐκ τῶν υἱῶν Λευὶ
τὴν ἱερατείαν λαμβάνοντες ἐντολὴν ἔχουσιν ἀποδεκατοῦν τὸν
λαὸν κατὰ τὸν νόμον, τοῦτ' ἐστιν τοὺς ἀδελφοὺς αὐτῶν, καίπερ
ἐξεληλυθότας ἐκ τῆς ὀσφύος ᾿Αβραάμ· 6. ὁ δὲ μὴ γενεαλογούμενος
ἐξ αὐτῶν δεδεκάτωκεν ᾿Αβραάμ, καὶ τὸν ἔχοντα τὰς ἐπαγγελίας
εὐλόγηκεν. 7. χωρὶς δὲ πάσης ἀντιλογίας τὸ ἔλαττον ὑπὸ τοῦ
κρείττονος εὐλογεῖται. 8. καὶ ὧδε μὲν δεκάτας ἀποθνῄσκοντες
ἄνθρωποι λαμβάνουσιν, ἐκεῖ δὲ μαρτυρούμενος ὅτι ζῇ. 9. καὶ
ὡς ἔπος εἰπεῖν, δι' ᾿Αβραὰμ καὶ Λευὶ ὁ δεκάτας λαμβάνων
δεδεκάτωται, 10. ἔτι γὰρ ἐν τῇ ὀσφύϊ τοῦ πατρὸς ἦν ὅτε
συνήντησεν αὐτῷ Μελχισέδεκ.

Heb 7:10 presents few text-critical problems of any great
importance. In those cases where extant alternative readings
exist, consideration of the relevant criteria leads without
difficulty to the probable original reading.

The variant ὅς in vs. 1, in spite of stronger manuscript
data (א A B Cᶜ D I K 17, 33, al.), is to be rejected on
internal grounds in favor of ὁ συναντήσας (p⁴⁶ C* Byz). The
former reading, which introduces either a pointless anacoluthon
or a stylistically inferior parenthesis (ὅς . . . ἐμέρισεν
᾿Αβραάμ), is best explained as a primitive reduplication of
the initial σ of the following word.[1] Several emendations
to vss. 1-2(a), being poorly attested homiletic glosses suggested by the Genesis narrative, warrant no serious atten-

---

1) B.F. Westcott and F.J.A. Hort, *The New Testament in the Original
Greek* (2 vols.; Cambridge & London, 1881), II, appendix, 130.

tion. For example, a later hand amplified the phrase "re-turning from the slaughter of the kings" with the spurious addendum, "because he pursued the foreigners and rescued Lot with all the captivity." In vs. 2 p[46] and B support the singular παντός as an alternative reading to the preferred πάντων. In the same verse p[46], a few versions and Latin fathers wrongly omit δὲ καί after the adverb ἔπειτα. Manu-scripts with the exception of D*424**, 1739 rightly retain οὗτος in vs. 4 after πηλίκος. Οὗτος may have been omitted by virtue of its identical termination as the preceding word. Its retention in the text heightens the force of the clause.[1] Textual authority for the insertion of καί after ᾧ (ℵ A C D[c] E[c] K L Vulg[codd] Syr[hkl] Arm Chrys Cyr TR) in the same verse is only slightly inferior to that which omits the particle (p[46] B D* E* 1739 Vulg[arm] It Syr[pes] Cop[boh] Ambr). It is preferable to suppose that a later copyist added the parti-cle on the basis of the ᾧ καὶ combination in vs. 2.

---

1) As in the AV ("Consider how great this man was . . .") and the NASB, against the RSV ("See how great he is!") and the NEB which may reflect the shorter reading.

III. OVERVIEW OF THE TEXT

Before representing the history of interpretation, a preliminary survey of the text and an identification of its
exegetical problems is necessary. In order to demonstrate
the superiority of the New Covenant to the Old and thus to
forestall the reversion of his readers to Judaism and its
cultus, the writer of Hebrews constructed a series of arguments which culminates in ch. 7 in a declaration of the superiority of the priesthood of Jesus to that of Aaron. The
priesthood of the Son is alluded to in ch. 2:17, 18 and ch.
4:14-16, and its specifically Melchizedekian character is
affirmed in ch. 5:6, 10. With the foundation thus laid, the
writer was set for a detailed explication of the excellence
of Jesus' Melchizedekian priesthood in contrast with the
antiquated Levitical order. But conscious of the dullness
and immaturity of his readers, the author inserted a para-
netic digression (ch. 5:11-6:19) to prepare them for higher
teaching concerning the distinctive and unique Melchizedekian
order of priesthood. In Heb 7:1-10 the writer initially unfolds the significance of Melchizedek, the ancient priestly
model or type of Christ before developing in vss. 11-28 the
theology of the true high priest who would arise after "the
likeness of Melchizedek." The argument of Hebrews 7 thus
advances in logical and precise sequence from the typical
priestly figure of antiquity to the antitypical heavenly
high priest of the New Covenant.
Heb 7:1-10, then, focuses on the excellence of Melchizedek, his person and his priesthood. By means of a subtle
exposition of the Genesis narrative the royal and priestly
figure from the dark reaches of antiquity is portrayed as
king of righteousness and peace who is devoid of parentage,
descent, commencement and termination of life. In a certain
respect he is likened to the Son of God himself. The conclusion which the writer draws is that the ancient priest-
king of the highest God continues in priesthood for ever
(vss. 1-3). Thereafter Melchizedek's threefold superiority
to the patriarch Abraham and hence to the Levites descended
from him is deduced from the data of the Genesis record:

(i) Melchizedek received tithes from Abraham (vss. 4-6a);
(ii) Melchizedek bestowed the blessing upon Abraham (vss.
6b-7); and (iii) the Levitical priests succumbed to death
whereas Melchizedek "lives on" (vs. 8). Heb 7:1-10 thus unfolds the new and profound concept of priesthood "after the
order of Melchizedek."

Before proceeding to the interpretation of Heb 7:1-10 in
history, it is necessary to identify the leading exegetical
issues of the text in greater detail. A distinctive feature
of Hebrews' argumentation is the manner in which single
pregnant texts are stressed, interspersed with discourse of
lesser moment. The importance of Psa 110:4 to the writer
effectively ensures that the principal features of the argument focus about the idea of the timelessness of the new
priestly order. The fact of the absolute eternity of the
Melchizedekian order of priesthood was stated in ch. 5:10
and 6:20 and is now worked out in detail in ch. 7. Hence the
motif of the *eternity* of Melchizedek and of the priesthood
he exercises constitutes the prominent theme of the text
before us.

The writer's apparent selective recitation and interpretation of the Gen 14:17-20 pericope raises several questions
in respect of the person and priestly dignity of Melchizedek:
(i) Who was the furtive figure portrayed in the primitive
record, and what significance do we attach to his mysterious
appearance in the primal history (vss. 1 ff.)? (ii) How are
we to understand the writer's representation of Melchizedek
in terms of the alpha-privative triad, ἀπάτωρ, ἀμήτωρ,
ἀγενεαλόγητος, in the great exegetical conundrum of the text
(vs. 3)? (iii) In what sense can it be affirmed that Melchizedek is endowed with μήτε ἀρχὴν ἡμερῶν μήτε ζωῆς τέλος (vs.
3)? (iv) What points of correspondence did the writer seek
to establish between the two priestly figures by means of
the NT *hapax legomenon* ἀφομοιοῦν (vs. 3)? Alternatively, if
Melchizedek is regarded as a figure or type of Christ, which
of the statements made in respect of Melchizedek apply to
the antitype? (v) What did the writer intend to convey by
the affirmation that Melchizedek μένει ἱερεὺς εἰς τὸ διηνεκές
(vs. 3)? The four declarations of vs. 3 are by no means
self-evident and have been subjected to an extensive vari-

ety of interpretations. If the statements are interpreted
in a strictly literal sense, Melchizedek would appear as a
supra-human figure whose priesthood would encroach upon the
eternal priesthood of Christ. Because of its importance to
the argument of the text vs. 3 will necessarily occupy a
prominent place in the history. (vi) Are we justified in
applying the extraordinary ascription ὅτι ζῆ to Melchizedek,
or did the writer thereby intend to portray Christ himself
(vs. 8)? If properly descriptive of Melchizedek, does the
phrase pertain to his person or to the perpetuation of his
priestly office? (vii) In view of *religionsgeschichtlich*
interest in the Melchizedek motif, particularly during the
past hundred years, it will be necessary to reflect upon
the extent to which Jewish and pagan extra-biblical conceptions may have stimulated the writer's development of Melchizedek as chief ministrant of the new order of priesthood.

IV. THE HISTORY OF INTERPRETATION

1. AGE OF THE REFORMATION

(a) Humanistic Interpretation

The school of biblical humanism at the turn of the sixteenth century represents a clearly defined transition between mediaeval and Reformation exegesis. Embracing the
spirit of the Renaissance with its emphasis upon the language and literature of antiquity, the humanists stimulated
scholarly inquiry into the NT documents. Inspired by the
genius of Erasmus, the movement sought to get behind the
venerated Latin Vulgate to the neglected Greek text. Repu-
diating the exegetical infallibility of the Pope, the Christian humanists sought via independent philological and literary investigations to determine the precise meaning of
the text as intended by the author. From there the message
of the text was set forth in forms convenient and intelli-
gible to the reader, hence the appearance of paraphrases,
annotations and explanations of the NT documents.

The labors of Desiderius Erasmus (1466-1536), the renowned
Dutch humanist and Augustinian theologian, signaled a new
era in the interpretation of the NT. Erasmus perceived that
the true message of Scripture was occluded by the multiple-
sense schema of mediaeval exegesis from which issued forth
fruitless disputations, moral platitudes and theological
hairsplitting. The domination of biblical studies by dogma,
together with a thoroughgoing neglect of philology and the
absence of historical foundations, compelled Erasmus to return to the Greek text of the NT and to elucidate its meaning from the rules of grammar, the historical setting of
the passage and the immediate context. In 1516 amidst a
storm of controversy, Erasmus produced a new Latin version
of the NT which was intended to supplant the 'inspired'
Vulgate. Together with the new Latin translation appeared
the first published edition of the Greek Testament which,
although primitive by modern standards, was a milestone in
biblical studies. Later learned annotations were appended

to the new Latin version.[1] Erasmus' other notable contribution appeared in 1522 in the form of paraphrases of the NT
books.[2] Intended to restate the mind of the author and unfold the connection of ideas, the paraphrases fulfilled a
need unmet by the traditional mediaeval glosses and scholia.
Thus Erasmus delivered a serious blow to scholastic interpretation and emerged a distant precursor of a truly scientific hermeneutic.

In his exposition of our text Erasmus makes no mention
of the traditional Roman Catholic dogma that Melchizedek's
bread and wine 'offering' is a type of the Eucharist. Melchizedek's significance consists in the fact that the "mystical Psalm" portrays the ancient priest-king as a shadow
or type of Christ. Guided by classical philology, Erasmus
renders ἀπάτωρ, ἀμήτωρ, ἀγενεαλόγητος as "ignoti patris,
ignotae matris, ignoti generis," implying that Melchizedek's
ancestors were of such obscure or humble station that his
family register was unable to be given up. But behind the
bare literal sense of the words Erasmus detects a spiritual
sense rich in Christological content: "everything to this
point agrees with Christ our high priest . . . who, with
respect to his deity, had neither father on earth nor mother,
whose pedigree no man can declare, who had neither beginning
nor shall have end, and whose priesthood continues for ever."
Erasmus' deviation from the common interpretation of the
fathers--"'without father,' on earth as regards Jesus'
humanity; 'without mother,' in heaven as regards his deity"--
reflects his depreciation of the humanity of Christ. That
is, the Christian humanist had an imperfect understanding
of Christ's divinity and humanity united in the God-man.

Jacob Faber Stapulensis (c. 1450-1536),[3] the French humanist and biblical scholar, prepared the ground for Reformation hermeneutics by returning to the biblical sources and
abandoning the multiple-sense schema of mediaeval exegesis.
His unwavering external loyalty to the Roman Church is re-

---

1) *Novum Testamentum cum adnotationibus*, vol. VI of *D. Erasmi opera
omnia*, ed. J. Le Clerc (10 vols.; Lugdunum Batavorum, 1703-7), 1001 ff.
2) *Paraphrases in Novum Testamentum*, vol. VII of *opera omnia*, 1176 ff.
3) *Pauli apostoli epistolae* (Parisius, 1515), 237 ff.

flected in an exegesis of our text which deviates far less
from traditional Catholic interpretation than does that of
the more independently minded Erasmus.

Heb 7:1-10 established Melchizedek as a perfect figure of
Christ not only via the dual titles "king of righteousness,"
"king of peace" and the historical incidents of his blessing
Abraham and receiving the tithes, but chiefly insofar as
the royal priest of Salem offered bread and wine in anticipation of the perpetual sacrifice of the Mass. Although both
Melchizedek and Christ exercise a universal priesthood which
is far more excellent than the particular Jewish ministration, the priesthood and sacrifice of Christ stands above
the priesthood and sacrifice of Melchizedek, since Christ
offers to God no earthly morsels but heavenly bread and heavenly wine in the form of his own body and blood. The Salemite's
bread and wine offering to God in celebration of Abraham's
rout of the four kings thus constitutes the ground of Christ's
title, priest "according to the *ritus* and *oblatio* of Melchizedek."

By concealing mention of Melchizedek's parentage, genealogy, beginning and termination of life, the Holy Spirit
established a further correspondence between the two priestly figures. In terms of Christ, ἀπάτωρ characterizes his
human nature, ἀμήτωρ his divine nature, whereas ἀγενεαλόγητος
signifies that his generation from the Father is ineffable
and incomprehensible. Stapulensis devotes a lengthy excursus to a refutation of objections that Christ could not be
"without genealogy" since his lineage from Abraham is carefully traced in Matthew's Gospel. The Catholic humanist
argues that in a sense Christ both possesses and does not
possess a genealogical register. On the one hand Christ's
lineage is fully verifiable; on the other hand, by virtue
of the sacrament of the incarnation, his descent remains
completely unknown and unknowable. But since the humanity
and divinity are intermingled in the Son and ineffable deity
vastly overshadows mundane humanity, the antitypical Melchizedek properly may be regarded as ἀγενεαλόγητος.

(b) The Protestant Reformers

Like Erasmus the Protestant reformers rejected the mediaeval fourfold meaning of Scripture in favor of the literal
sense. They renounced dependence upon the judgments of the
fathers and paid close attention to the Hebrew and Greek
texts of Scripture. Yet the reformers elevated the study of
the Bible beyond the biblical humanists' regard for the literature of classical antiquity. Indeed, their interpretation of the Bible was shaped by deep-seated religious and
theological concerns rather than by peripheral literary and
aesthetic interests. Furthermore, they placed great stress
upon the centrality of Christ in Scripture, the whole of
divine revelation pointing to him. Reformation interpretation of our text was flavored by a vigorous anti-papal polemic directed against the notion of the iterated sacrifice
of Christ in the Mass and against the Roman clerical order.
During the Reformation, then, exegesis, dogmatics and polem-
ics were brought together for the purpose of extolling Christ
and the gospel.

The lectures of Martin Luther (1483-1586) on the Epistle
to the Hebrews[1] were delivered early in his career at Wittenberg shortly before his Ninety-five Theses were published
in October, 1517. Luther's university lectures on Hebrews
were expounded by means of the mediaeval technique of glosses and scholia, an interpretive form which the celebrated
Doctor later abandoned. Luther patently refuted the scholastic fourfold exegetical schema, insisting on the plain
or grammatico-historical sense of the text.[2] The reformer's
exposition of Scripture reflects a brilliant marriage of
dogma, polemic and homiletic exhortation. Yet it is clear
that Luther superimposed upon the bare, literal sense of
the text a deeper spiritual meaning not unlike the Roman

---

1) "Divi Pauli apostoli ad Hebraeos epistola," *WA*, LVII, iii, 36 ff.
(glosses), 188 ff. (scholia).
2) Refuting the Roman Catholic assertion that the Mass was prefigured
by Melchizedek's "sacrifice" of bread and wine, Luther affirms: "Perhaps
someone could contrive out of this the allegory that just as Melchizedek
brings out bread and wine, so Christ brings out the bread of life and
the wine of joy, that is, the Holy Spirit with his gifts. But allego-
ries of this sort prove nothing . . . . It is hazardous to change the
meanings in this way and to depart so far from the literal meaning."
On Gen 14:18. *WA*, XLII, 539.

Catholic *sensus plenior*. From there it was only a short
step to the corollary affirmation that via illumination of
the Spirit, the interpreter perceives Christ by faith in all
of Scripture. This radical Christocentric approach to the
biblical text is reflected in Luther's celebrated maxim:
"Christus est punctus mathematicus sacrae scripturae."[1]

The powerfully dogmatic character of Luther's interpretation is manifest in his exposition of the figure of Melchizedek in our text. The attributes "righteousness" and
"peace" (vs. 2) have principal reference to *divine righteousness*, "the very grace by which a man is justified," and *divine peace* which is uniquely "hidden under the cross . . .
just as the sun is hidden under a cloud." This suggests that
Luther ventures to interpret the OT in the light of the NT,
and particularly the Melchizedek motif in the light of the
justification doctrine of St. Paul. Affirming the Christ-
centeredness of all Scripture, Luther argues that the titles
"king of righteousness" and "king of peace" are ascribed to
Melchizedek only because in precisely these matters he represents the Son of God as everlasting king. Luther's chief
concern in explicating Heb 7:1-10 is to elicit the fourfold
superiority of *Christ* and his priesthood. Clearly Luther's
exegesis is dominated by his rigid law-gospel antithesis.
(i) Christ surpasses the legal order because of his *eternal
existence*, the reality of which was prefigured through Melchizedek whose parentage, genealogy and commencement of life
are all unrecorded (vs. 3). In his later exposition of Psalm
110 (1535), Luther elaborates on the theme of the eternity
of the type and antitype.

> As there is no record concerning the father and mother
> of this Melchizedek, his beginning and end (the mean-
> ing is not that Melchizedek had no father and mother,
> but that there is no record of them), just so Christ,
> of whom Melchizedek is a type, is truly a priest of
> this sort. He had no beginning, and he will have no
> end. From all eternity he is, and unto all eternity he
> will remain.[2]

(ii) Christ's priesthood is superior to that of Levi because
of the *blessing* bestowed upon Abraham (vss. 6, 7). What was

---

1) *Tischreden*, ed. K. Drescher (6 vols.; Weimar, 1912-21), II, 439.
2) *WA*, XLI, 178.

the nature of Melchizedek's blessing? Luther's exposition
of the Psalm citation is laden with Reformation distinctives.

> Melchizedek is not merely a type or picture of Christ
> and his priesthood, but one who has actually exercised
> that very same office as a preacher of the gospel. For
> this reason he was also called a priest of God before
> Aaron's priestly office as a proclamation of the for-
> giveness of his sins and of the assurance of God's
> help and grace.[1]

(iii) Christ surpasses the legal priests because of the *perpetuity* of his life (vs. 8). Abraham and Levi succumbed to
death, but Christ lives on endlessly. Preoccupied with the
Christological implications of the text, Luther fails even
to mention Melchizedek in the scholia to this verse. Yet in
a gloss to the text of vs. 8 he affirms that Melchizedek
"lives on" in the sense that his death is unrecorded in
Scripture.

(iv) The final evidence for Christ's superiority to the legal order consists in Melchizedek's *reception of tithes* from
Abraham and hence from Levi also (vss. 4, 6). Why was Levi
judged to have paid tithes to Melchizedek and not Christ
himself? Responding to this question Luther betrays a resid-
ual interest in allegory by appropriating the interpretation of Peter Lombard.

> Christ did not pay tithes along with Levi, although He
> was with Levi in the loins of Abraham; for He was not
> in the loins of Abraham according to the same law. For
> Levi was there according to the law of carnal concupis-
> cence, but Christ was there according to the law of love.

Thus it is clear from Luther's exposition of Heb 7:1-10 that
the reformer focuses much less attention upon the historical
Melchizedek than upon the person of Christ. This is consistent with his interpretive maxim that the exegete ought to
approach Scripture "with spiritual eyes,"[2] with the result
that "everything in the Scriptures signifies and points
principally to the promised Christ."[3]

But who in reality was Melchizedek? The scholia--the continuous albeit spiritualized exposition of the text--affords
no insight into his identity; it is concerned entirely with

---

1) *WA*, XLI, 187, 188.
2) On Psa 110:4. *WA*, XLI, 174.
3) *WA*, XLI, 175.

the antitype. But in the glosses--the marginal or interlinear insertions in the text--Luther affirms a preference for the traditional Jewish view that Melchizedek was Shem, the most pious of Noah's sons. Melchizedek admirably corresponds with Shem, first, because of the latter's *longevity*. The archpatriarch Shem lived fully 500 years beyond the flood and survived Abraham by some thirty-five years. Shem was also reputed for his patent *uprightness* in the discharge of civil (kingly) and religious (priestly) duties. Indeed, Shem merited distinction in the latter sphere, for "he gained a reputation for righteousness because of his service in the church; for he taught the forgiveness of sins through the future seed of the woman."[1] Finally, Luther observes that Melchizedek agrees with Shem because of his *dignity*. The reformer elaborates the point by suggesting that "after his father Noah . . . Shem was without a doubt the chief and true pope."[2]

Ulrich Zwingli (1484-1531), the pioneer reformer in German Switzerland, wrote brief expositions of all the books of the Bible. Select theological treatises on Reformation themes offer a useful supplement to his all too sparse comments on the biblical text. Zwingli affirms in his commentary on Hebrews[3] that the apostle's mystical interpretation of Melchizedek's name, title and life-data establish the Salemite monarch as an eloquent figure of Christ. However, explication of the basis of the typological correspondence is set forth more fully in a polemical treatise[4] in which Zwingli vigorously attacks the Roman Catholic contention that Melchizedek resembles Christ (ἀφωμοιωμένος κτλ) chiefly in that he sacrificed bread and wine in celebration of Abraham's rout of the hostile kings. The reformer has only contempt for the traditional syllogism of Catholic interpretation:

Melchizedek, as priest of the Most High, offered a

---

1) On Gen 14:18. *WA*, XLII, 536.
2) On Psa 110:4. *WA*, XLI, 176.
3) "In epistolam beati Pauli ad Hebraeos expositio," *opera* (4 vols.; Tiguri, 1581), IV, 573 ff.
4) "Christiana & orthodoxa responsio de idolis & missa," *opera*, I, 215 ff.

bread and wine sacrifice. But Christ is a priest "after
the order of Melchizedek." Therefore, Christ offers
himself in the Mass under the symbols of bread and wine.
"Who ever heard of or invented a more inept, feeble or ab-
surd argument?" Zwingli retorts. Following Abraham's defeat
of the four kings Melchizedek never brought a bread and wine
offering, either to Abraham or to God himself. Quite apart
from such sophistry, Zwingli argues that the biblical text
authorizes Melchizedek as a threefold type of Christ thus:
the Salemite is acclaimed (i) "king of righteousness" and
(ii) "king of peace," in addition to which, (iii) the details
of his descent, birth and decease are all unknown. Not only
are the facts of Melchizedek's origin a mystery, but the
man himself was known to no one, being a foreigner and an
alien. Hence the principal emphasis of Heb 7:1 ff. is not
sacramental (Zwingli's concept of the Eucharist would have
made this doubly difficult), but it is more properly Christological: "Christ's birth, by which he assumed human flesh,
is inexpressible and thus far transcends the power of human
reason. Wherefore it truly follows that the priesthood of
Christ is eternal."

The monumental contributions to theological science by
John Calvin (1509-64) are enshrined in his biblical commentaries and in the *Institutio christianae religionis*, his
systematic exposition of the whole of Christian doctrine.
Calvin's main interpretive presupposition, that the task of
the exegete is to "unfold the mind of the writer" with "lu-
cid brevity" (*perspicua brevitas*),[1] is reflected both in his
commentaries and in the *Institutio*. In addition to faith-
fully reproducing the intent of the author, Calvin's writings
display a deep penetration into the religious significance
of Scripture and are characterized, for the most part, by
an avoidance of lengthy digressions which only detract from
continuity of exposition.

Calvin approaches Heb 7:1-10[2] as he does all Scripture
with the aim of discovering Christ portrayed therein.[3] Thus

---

1) Dedicatory letter to Simon Grynaeus, prefaced to Calvin's commentary on Romans. *CR*, XXXVIII, 402.
2) "Commentarius in epistolam ad Hebraeos," *CR*, LXXXIII, 82 ff.
3) Note his comment on Jn 5:39. *CR*, LXXV, 125: "Therefore it must

the several affirmations about the Salemite king are viewed
as purely typological statements whose complete meaning is
realized when applied to the person of Christ. Although Melchizedek was divinely ordained a type of the Son of God and
on that account must have embodied the highest moral virtues,
in the final analysis the titles "king of righteousness"
and "king of peace" (vs. 2) properly can be attributed only
to Christ. He alone imputes to the faithful the judicial
righteousness of God and grants to those so reconciled the
favor of a conscience set at peace with God.

The predicates ἀπάτωρ, ἀμήτωρ are elucidated by the following term, ἀγενεαλόγητος, from which Calvin concludes that
the apostle "exempts Melchizedek from what is common to
others, a descent by birth; by which he means that he is
eternal, so that his beginning from men was not to be sought
after." Melchizedek was begotten by human parents, but Calvin hastens to add: "Now as the Holy Spirit in mentioning
this king, the most illustrious of his age, is wholly silent
as to his birth, and makes afterwards no record of his death,
is not this the same thing as though eternity was to be
ascribed to him?" Melchizedek thus appears in Scripture as
a model of the eternal Christ, for "while Scripture sets
forth to us Melchizedek as one who had never been born and
never died, it shows to us as in a mirror, that Christ has
neither a beginning nor an end."[1] This principle is further
illustrated in vs. 8 where silence about Melchizedek's
death is construed as evidence of his life. Even though Melchizedek ultimately perished, the statement of his immortality remains valid because, in the final analysis, it is

---

first be said that Christ is not duly known from any other source than
from the Scriptures. But if this is so, it follows that the Scriptures
must be read in the expectation that we discover Christ therein."

1) In Calvin's homiletic exposition of the Melchizedek motif great
prominence is given to the soteriological implications of the phrase
μήτε ἀρχὴν ημερῶν κτλ: "He is without beginning and without end; without beginning in that he is God eternal and without end in that we have
eternal life in him. As it is said in the prophet Isaiah, 'as for his
generation, who considered that he was cut off out of the land of the
living, stricken for the transgression of my people?' The Church is
immortal through the virtue of our Lord Jesus Christ; thus he is with
even greater reason without end." "Trois sermons sur l'histoire de
Melchisedec," *CR*, LI, 649.

descriptive of the Son of God himself.

The Christological conclusions deduced from the Melchizedek motif illustrate a characteristic of Calvin's exegesis.
The reformer insists that a correct understanding of the
mind of the writer is achieved by renouncing allegorical
exegesis and by insisting upon the "sensus literalis" of the
text. This is further defined as the "sensus genuinus" or
"sensus versus,"[1] the spiritual sense conveyed via illumination of the Spirit.[2] As with Luther, the practical result
of Calvin's exposition of our text is an overshadowing of
the independent reality of Melchizedek by the antitype
through a profoundly Christological exegesis. Calvin supports
this judgment when he remarks: "Melchizedek is not to be
considered here in his private capacity, but as a sacred
type of Christ." Indeed, Calvin refers to the Christological conclusions deduced from vss. 3 and 8 as great "spiritual
mysteries of God."

Clearly Calvin's explication of the Melchizedek-Christ
typology centers upon the respective persons rather than
upon the priestly offices they exercise. Perhaps as a mute
polemic against the Roman clerical order Calvin minimizes
Melchizedek's role as a ministering priest.

Exegesis of the text is supplemented by occasional out-
bursts of polemic by which Calvin refutes the dogma and
praxis of the Roman Church. In the spirit of the Reformation
Calvin contests the Catholic contention that Melchizedek's
presentation of bread and wine prefigured the Mass, wherein
the sacrifice of Jesus is reenacted. How "detestable, therefore, is the fiction of those who, not content with the
priesthood of Christ, have dared to take it upon themselves
to sacrifice him, a thing attempted in the Papacy, where
the Mass is represented as an immolation of Christ."[3] In his
sermons on Genesis 14, Psalm 110 and Hebrews 7, Calvin's
denunciation of the Mass is even more vitriolic.

It is a pity that the Devil's power has been so great
that for 1400 years he has so blinded those who called

---

1) On Gal 4:22. *CR*, LXXVIII, 236 ff.
2) *Institutio* I.7.4. *CR*, XXX, 59.
3) *Institutio* II.15.6. *CR*, XXX, 367.

themselves Christians that on this matter they have
invented a devilish fantasy that Christ was prefigured
in the person of Melchizedek and that his body is the
heavenly bread and his blood the wine to feed souls
and that he offered both. At first blush this allegory
will please those who have itching ears; . . . But it
is no question here of an offering made to God. Moses
said that Melchizedek king of Salem offered bread and
wine, that is to say, he gave it to Abraham.[1]

(c) Socinian Interpreters

The Italian theologians Lelius Socinus (1525-62) and his
nephew Faustus Socinus (1539-1604) are remembered as forerunner and founder, respectively, of the rationalistic antitrinitarian movement which arose out of the soil of sixteenth
century Catholicism. These early theologians were followed
by their Unitarian descendants in rejecting the plurality
of persons and community of nature within the Godhead. In
consequence, Jesus was acclaimed a mortal man whose humanity
was endowed with extraordinary virtue. Only after his resurrection and exaltation, and by virtue of the divine power
bestowed on him, could Christ be regarded as a divine and
immortal figure. The orthodox terminology but heterodox content of Socinian teaching stimulated a firm ecclesiastical
reaction against the movement which impelled the Socinians,
who had been active in Italy, Switzerland and Germany to
seek sanctuary in neighboring Poland. In time Raków emerged
as the spiritual and intellectual center of the society
which produced in the seventeenth century such articulate
antitrinitarian proponents as Johann Crell (1590-1631) and
Jonas Schlichting (1592-1661).

Member of a noble Roman Catholic Sienese family, Faustus
Socinus through the instruction of his uncle Lelius became
increasingly disenchanted with the doctrinal platform of
both the Roman Catholic Church and the Protestant reformers.
In 1575 Socinus left his native Italy and took up residence
in Basel where he devoted himself to extensive theological
study and writing. Later he became actively involved in
antitrinitarian activities in Transylvania before hostile

---

1) *CR*, LI, 660.

reaction forced him to flee to Poland and Lithuania where
he sought to consolidate the various antitrinitarian parties
which had arisen. Socinus never wrote a commentary on Hebrews,
but he expounded our text in several theological treatises
concerned with the priesthood of Christ (which the Socinians
regarded as but an adjunct of his kingship[1]).

Hebrews' exposition of Melchizedek was intended to demonstrate how that in earliest times Christ's priesthood or
kingship was foreshadowed by the Salemite priest-king.
Socinus' inability to accept Jesus' divinity and his rejection of the existence of any ontological relationship between the latter and the God of the Bible, precluded his
interpreting the statements of vs. 3 in terms of the persons
of Melchizedek and Christ. Thus the antitrinitarian expressly refutes the traditional interpretation that Melchizedek's
representation as ἀπάτωρ, ἀμήτωρ suggests that Christ was
in some sense devoid of father and mother. Likewise Socinus
denies that μήτε ἀρχὴν ἡμερῶν κτλ implies the absence of
beginning or end of Christ's personal existence. Vs. 3 is
concerned not with the persons of the two figures but with
their respective priestly offices. Thus Socinus affirms:

> When in vs. 3 Melchizedek is compared with Christ, the
> resemblance is not general and universal but insofar
> as he is king and priest, but especially as priest.
> Hence the words "nec initium dierum, etc." can in no
> wise be properly applied to the person of Christ, or
> Son of God. On the contrary, it is necessary that they
> be applied to his kingship, ie, to his priesthood.[2]

The former pair of epithets affirm no more than, as in the
case of the shadow, Jesus possessed no Aaronic priestly
pedigree. The latter expression suggests that Jesus neither
succeeded another nor was he himself succeeded in priest-

---

1) For a formal statement that Christ's priestly office was but a
function of his kingship, see the section "De Christi sacerdotio" in
"Christianae religionis institutio," *Socini opera omnia* (2 vols.;
Irenopolis, 1656), I, 664. In the English translation of the *Catechesis
racoviensis* (the document based largely on the manuscripts of Faustus
Socinus), explication of the prophetic office of Christ fills 180 pages.
Consideration of the priestly office of Christ occupies only some ten
pages. *The Racovian Catechism*, trans. Thomas Rees (London, 1818).
2) "Responsio ad libellum Jacobi Wuieki de divinitate filii Dei &
spiritus sancti," *Socini opera*, II, 609.

hood.[1] Socinus further insists that μένει ἱερεὺς κτλ in no
sense implies that, following Melchizedek, Jesus always was
and always will be endowed with priestly dignity. The Socinian argues at length that Christ undertook the exercise of
priesthood (so-called) only after his bloodletting on the
cross and ascension. Socinus argues from the analogy of the
twofold work of the Aaronic high priest: (i) the spilling
of the blood of the victim, and (ii) the application of the
blood in the holy of holies. Only after the death of the
victim did the Aaronic high priest enter the innermost shrine
to effect the expiation of sins. By analogy Socinus distin-
guishes between Christ's bloodletting ("fusio sanguinus")
and his sacrifice proper ("oblatio"). The former occurred
on earth, was a necessary preparation for the exercise of
priestly service, but of itself possessed no expiatory power. The latter transpired in the heavenly world and, being
the presentation of the fruit of Christ's passion to the
Most High, constitutes the means by which the expiation of
man's ignorance and misdeeds is effected.[2]

Only Schlichting among the older Socinians undertook to
write a commentary on Hebrews.[3] Johann Crell, who wrote numerous exegetical works on the NT, had an essential share
in the work. Schlichting presided over a prominent Raków
parish but was forced to flee Poland during the severe anti-
Socinian reaction which set in towards the middle of the
seventeenth century. His Hebrews commentary evinces many
characteristics of a learned and scientific treatment of
the biblical text, but his exegesis is overlaid with a deep
stratum of antitrinitarian dogma and polemic.

Socinian dogma emerges when Schlichting expresses prefer-

---

1) "Explicationes variorum sacrae scripturae locorum," *Socini opera*,
I, 151.
2) "Christianae religionis institutio," *Socini opera*, I, 664. "De
Jesu Christi filii Dei natura," *Ibid.* II, 392: "Christ did not offer
himself to God on the cross but only in heaven itself. This is amply
supported by the fact that Christ was not properly inaugurated to
priesthood until after his death, indeed, until after his ascension to
heaven. . . . Thus we understand that Christ was not truly priest before
he had attained to the glorification of his body and to immortality."
3) *Commentarius in epistolam ad Hebraeos* (Racovia, 1634); repr. in
Crellii opera omnia (4 vols.; Eleutheropolis, 1656), II, 130 ff.

ence for the word "princeps" as a synonym for ἱερεύς (vs. 1).
The epithets "king of righteousness" and "king of peace"
(vs. 2) display an elegant affinity to Christ who in truth
is "rex omnium justissimus" and "maxime pacificus." The Socinian departs from the pronounced soteriological emphasis
of traditional interpretation by affirming, for example, that
Christ is "king of peace" inasmuch as he embodies the spirit
of true pacificism unlike the bellicose kings of this world.

Vs. 3 highlights a threefold resemblance between the
priestly offices of Melchizedek and Christ. Schlichting's
exegesis reflects a salutary consciousness of the independent reality of the Salemite priest-king, in comparison with
older Roman Catholic and Protestant interpretation which
tended to view vss. 2 and 3 primarily in terms of Christ.
(i) ἀπάτωρ, ἀμήτωρ, ἀγενεαλόγητος affirms that Melchizedek
acceded to sacerdotal office independently of priestly parentage and descent. The priesthood of Christ, Melchizedek's
antitype, is likewise unrelated to the priestly line of
Levi. (ii) Just as Melchizedek had neither predecessor nor
successor in office (μήτε ἀρχὴν ἡμερῶν κτλ), so the priesthood of Christ admits no rivals. (iii) Both Melchizedek and
Christ were endowed with an eternal priesthood, the perpetuity of Melchizedek's ministration being understood in
terms of the eternity attributed to the antitypical order
by Psa 110:4. Socinian presuppositions concerning the duration of Christ's priestly ministry exercise a determinative
effect upon the exegesis. Christ is said to be an eternal
priest in the sense that "his priesthood continues for the
longest time, indeed, for as long as there shall be scope
for the discharge of priestly functions or until the state
of affairs shall be altered, in which case there would be no
further need for his priesthood." According to Schlichting,
scope for the exercise of Christ's priesthood would exist
only during the earthly sojourn of the people of God. Subsequent to the elevation of the church there would be no
further need for the expiation of sins. Hence the *terminus
ad quem* of Jesus' priestly ministration is coincident with
the translation of the obedient community to heavenly immortality. As for the eternity ascribed to the type, Mel-

chizedek exercised priestly functions for a period of indef-
inite duration, ie, as long as the knowledge and worship of
the true God flourished amongst his subjects.

2. THE SEVENTEENTH CENTURY

(a) Roman Catholic Commentaries

The reforms initiated by Erasmus in the direction of a
scientific biblical exegesis were slow to be taken up by
post-Reformation Catholic exegetes. Instead interpreters of
the period continued to expound the multiple senses of Scripture and to draw heavily upon the interpretive judgments of
the fathers. During the post-Reformation ecclesiastical controversies interpretation was dominated by harsh polemic
against theologians of the Lutheran and Reformed parties.
Seventeenth century Catholic exegesis of our text was laden
with lengthy excurses reaffirming traditional views on the
sacrifice of the Mass and the Roman priesthood. The sum of
this dogma, polemic and exegesis was brought together in
massive compilations on the Pauline corpus, the majority of
which have proved to be of less value to posterity than, for
example, Reformed commentaries of the period.

With little of lasting worth accomplished by non-Prot-
estant interpreters during the sixteenth century, the works
of the Flemish exegete Cornelius a Lapide (1567-1637) stand
out as a tower of traditional Roman Catholic interpretation.
Professor of biblical exegesis for four decades, first at
the Louvain and then at the Roman College of Jesuits, a
Lapide wrote commentaries which long remained authorities
within the Catholic Church. The first of his volumenous
biblical commentaries to be published was a work on the
Pauline Epistles, the popularity of which is reflected by
the appearance of some eighty editions.[1] His interpretation
is characterized by an exhaustive defense and refutation of
alien intrusions upon orthodox Catholic dogma. A further
characteristic is the selective utilization of the mediaeval
fourfold scheme of exegesis--the literal sense propounding
the bare meaning of the words of the text and the allegorical, tropological and anagogical senses portraying, respectively, the theological, moral and eschatological mean-

---

1) Edn. consulted: *Commentaria in omnes divi Pauli epistolas* (Antwerpa, 1627), 887 ff.

ings for the full edification of the reader.[1]

A Lapide detects in our text "a sublime, subtle and allegorical discourse about Melchizedek" deduced from the
silence of the Genesis narrative. The *literal* sense of the
words "king of Salem" (vs. 1) implies that Melchizedek was
an historic ruler of Jerusalem who also exercised a priestly ministry. The *allegorical* meaning of the title points to
Christ who in the same holy city offered himself on the altar of the cross for the salvation of the world. The *anagogical* sense suggests that in Jerusalem the Messiah will
for ever administer a kingdom of justice and peace. At first
glance ἀπάτωρ, ἀμήτωρ, ἀγενεαλόγητος appear to suggest that
like some mysterious heavenly being Melchizedek suddenly
fell down to earth. The triad, in fact, represents Melchizedek insofar as (unlike other illustrious figures in the
OT) neither his father, mother nor descendants are detailed
in Scripture. Such mysterious omission of his ancestry suggests that the Canaanite prince who brought a bread and
wine sacrifice entered upon priestly office not by reason
of legal inheritance or carnal succession, but on the basis
of divine appointment. But "the principal and allegorical
reason" for omission of these details is that Melchizedek
might thereby be a fitting type of Christ. The correspondence
suggested by the foregoing triad is twofold:

> First, his father and mother are passed over in silence
> that thereby he might foreshadow Christ, who on earth
> as man is ἀπάτωρ, in heaven as God and Son of God is
> ἀμήτωρ. Second, . . . that it might be seen from his
> origin and birth that he would not be mortal but im-
> mortal and eternal . . . and thus a type of the eter-
> nity of Christ.

The phrase μένει ἱερεὺς κτλ highlights another typological correspondence in which the Mass figures significantly.
Melchizedek's priesthood is perpetual in that no one succeeded him in office. Similarly the priesthood of the antitype is eternal and that for two reasons: first on the God-
ward side, because of the perpetuity of Jesus' ministry of

---

1) See the section entitled: "Canones rerum in epistolas Pauli," particularly his sixth canon; *Commentaria*, 17. Therein a Lapide sets forth
the hermeneutical schema of Lyra: "littera gesta docet; quid credas
allegoria; moralis quid agas; quid speres anagogia."

intercession in heaven; second and even more significant, on the manward side, because "in his Church through his ministers, to be sure through priests appointed by him, Christ continually offers even to the end of the world the sacrifice of the Mass . . . wherein by divine power he effects the transubstantiation of the bread and wine into his body and blood." Thus from the statement of the text that Melchizedek "continue a priest for ever," a Lapide constructed an elaborate theological edifice founded upon Christ's perpetual administration of the Eucharist.

Wilhelm Estius (1542-1613) reflects a more independent exegetical stance in which traditional Roman Catholic emphases are moderated by the influence of Protestant biblical scholarship. Contrary to many Catholic contemporaries who indulged in a quest for hidden and obscure meanings, this scholar strove to elicit the plain sense of the text following the model of the Antiochene rather than the Alexandrian school of exegesis. His principal work, a highly esteemed commentary on the Pauline and Catholic Epistles,[1] first appeared in 1614 and was frequently reprinted through the nineteenth century.

Skillfully refuting the arguments of those who represented Melchizedek as a supra-human figure and Jewish opinion which identified him as Shem, Estius affirms that Melchizedek was a descendant of Ham, a prince and priest of the Canaanites. Estius follows Catholic interpretation which viewed Hebrews' portrait of Melchizedek as a typological representation deduced from the silence of the Genesis record. If ἀπάτωρ, ἀμήτωρ affirm that no mention is made in Holy Scripture of his father and mother, ἀγενεαλόγητος includes the additional notion that Scripture fails to enumerate Melchizedek's offspring or descendants, as if he had lived a celibate life. However, the ultimate reason why Melchizedek was so depicted was to convey higher spiritual truth about Christ.

> This indeed is favorable to the mysterious sense. For just as the eternity of Christ without beginning is denoted by the words ἀπάτωρ, ἀμήτωρ, so also his

---

1) Edn. consulted: *In omnes Pauli epistolas item in catholicas commentarii* (7 vols.; Moguntia, 1841-45), VI, 176 ff.

eternity without end is denoted by the term ἀγενεαλόγητος.[4]

This fundamental point of correspondence between Melchizedek
and Christ is reiterated by the words μήτε ἀρχὴν ἡμερῶν κτλ,
which the apostle again adduced from the silence of Scripture. The writer projects the absence of recorded birth and
death into the higher symbolic motif of the absolute eternity of the antitype. Estius observes how effectively vs.
3 refutes the error of the Arians who supposed that the Son
of God was created by the Father and thus could not have
been eternal *a parte ante*. Estius judges that Christ's designation as a Melchizedekian priest includes not only this
fundamental idea of absolute eternity but also the coordinate
notion (following the sacrifice of Melchizedek) of the offering of the body and blood of the Lord under the appearance
of bread and wine in the Mass.

The massive biblical commentaries of Augustus Calmet
(1672-1754), the French Benedictine monk,[2] long remained the
chief exegetical authority in the Catholic Church. Calmet,
who abandoned allegory in favor of the literal interpretation
of Scripture, was more an assiduous collector of exegetical
opinions from the past than a fresh innovator.

Moses' conscious suppression of the details of Melchizedek's life in Gen 14:18 ff. does not suggest that the latter was an obscure or insignificant figure, for one who would
later be likened to the Son of God must have been a man of
considerate eminence. The silence of Moses served to lay
the foundation for the later declaration of the apostle that
Melchizedek was an express type of the eternal generation,
divinity and unending priesthood of Christ. In respect of
his person,

> This silence is not without mystery. The author wished
> thereby to indicate that Jesus Christ would be father-

---

1) Estius rejects the interpretation that ἀπάτωρ, ἀμήτωρ signify absence of father and mother: "For how is Christ without father and without mother since he has a Father from eternity according to his divine
nature, and he received a mother in time according to his human nature?
How, I say, could he be without Father, when this very text names him
the Son of God?"
2) "Commentaire littéral sur l'Epître aux Hébreux," in *Commentaire
littéral sur les Epîtres de saint Paul* (2 vols.; Paris, 1716), II, 575 ff.

less on earth as man, motherless in heaven as God, and
without genealogy in that his origin is totally divine,
heavenly and ineffable.

In respect of his priesthood, the *argumentum e silentio* affirms that Christ neither inherited his priestly dignity nor
did he transmit it to another.

His priesthood is eternal, and does not terminate with
his death. Those who succeed him in office are no more
than his vice-regents. He is the Priest of priests,
and those whom he employs in the ministry exercise
only a small part of the priestly authority, the fullness of which resides in his person.

(b) Proponents of Lutheran Orthodoxy

During the century following the Protestant reformers,
Lutheran biblical interpretation gradually hardened into a
formalistic and quasi-scholastic system. Learned and doggedly
persistent theologians compiled massive, multi-volume compen-
dia of orthodox dogma which, although highly revered in their
day, have all but passed out of currency. Hence after the
Formula of Concord (1580), biblical exegesis became circum-
scribed by the narrow constraints of a rigidly dogmatic
confessional system. Rather than pursue fresh investigations
of their own, and intent upon preserving the ecclesiastical
status-quo, interpreters turned back the dissenting judgments of Roman Catholic, Socinian, Arminian or Calvinist
contemporaries with consummate zeal and dexterity. In particular, older Lutheran interpretation vigorously repudiated
the traditional Catholic eucharistic interpretation of the
Melchizedek pericope. Johann Gerhard (d. 1637), for example,
captions a lengthy excursus against Melchizedek's prefiguration of the 'sacrifice' of the Mass with the telling
title ἐκδίκησις ("vengeance").[1] Most Lutheran exegetes extracted from the text a mine of Christological truth by
means of the classical *argumentum e silentio*. For others,
Melchizedek's prefiguration of Christ was more dramatically
affirmed by identifying the Salemite ruler with Enoch,
Elijah or with Christ himself.

Giles Hunnius (1550-1603), the Tübingen-educated dog-

---

1) *Commentarius super epistolam ad Ebraeos* (Jaena, 1641), 161-67.

matician and exegete, was one of the leading Lutheran theologians of the latter half of the sixteenth century. In spirit, however, he is one with seventeenth century Lutheran orthodoxy. While holding the chair of theology at Wittenberg, he was instrumental in establishing the dominance of strict Lutheran orthodoxy which, during the following hundred years, produced a long succession of eminent theologians including Baldwin (d. 1627), Calov (d. 1686) and Quenstedt (d. 1688). In addition to numerous doctrinal and polemic works, Hunnius undertook the exposition of the entire NT.

In his Hebrews commentary[1] Hunnius observes that many of the unconverted among the Jews to whom the Epistle was directed were of the opinion that the Messiah was merely a human figure. The author counters this "destructive error" by sketching Melchizedek in such a fashion as to elegantly adumbrate the "eternal deity of Christ and his ineffable generation from the Father." The orthodox Lutheran emphasis upon the unity and communion of the two natures in the God-man is reflected in Hunnius' insistence that by design of the Holy Spirit ἀπάτωρ, ἀμήτωρ represent the humanity and the divinity of Christ united in one person. The former depicts Christ's divine and eternal generation from the Father, whereas the latter is an exact representation of the human nature of our Lord, "since from his mother alone without male seed was he begotten Christ the Lord." But on what basis did the author construct such an extraordinary argument? Hunnius discovers the interpretive key in vs. 8 which affirms of Melchizedek, ὅτι ζῇ. Furthermore, a link is detected between vs. 8 and the mention in Heb 11:5 of the translation of Enoch via divine power to eternal life. When viewed from the perspective of Enoch or Elijah who were elevated to life without passing through death, Melchizedek would most appropriately adumbrate the eternity of Christ and his priesthood. Thus:

> Without the imposition of death Melchizedek was translated to eternal life just as Enoch and Elijah, so that he might represent so much more suitably the perpetual

---

1) *Exegesis epistolae ad Hebraeos, scripta et recognita* (Francofurtum, 1586), 138 ff.

priesthood of Christ. The priestly order of the latter is eternal because after the manner and arrangement of Melchizedek he was appointed by the oath of God.

Lutheran orthodoxy attained its golden age in Abraham Calov (1612-1686), the influential dogmatician and exegete. Endowed with extraordinary energy, Calov published an enormous array of dogmatic, polemic, philosophical and exegetical works, many in special antagonism to Romanist, Arminian or Calvinist theologians. His principal dogmatic work, the twelve-volume *Systema locorum theologicorum*[1] is generally acclaimed one of the most significant dogmatic works of the period. Calov's primary exegetical work, the highly esteemed *Biblia illustrata*,[2] reflects a pervasively controversial flavor. In this massive commentary the annotations of Grotius serve as the basis of his exposition. Calov occasionally concurs with the exegesis of the Arminian, but more often expresses contempt for his views.[3]

A chief feature of Calov's exposition of our text is his concern to counter the Socinian and Arminian contention that vs. 3 describes the priestly offices of type and antitype rather than the priests themselves. Unwilling to accept such a bold reduction of a patent Christological text, Calov argues that "to be without parentage, descendants, beginning and end of life is not descriptive of a priesthood but of a real person." Calov himself advances a mystical, Christocentric interpretation of the alpha-privative triad in vs. 3: Christ is without mother as God, without father as man, and without genealogy both as God and man. The word ἀγενεαλόγητος is particularly rich in Christological content. The Holy Spirit characterized the God-man thus because

> his divine generation is not able to be comprehended by the human mind, nor can his human generation be known through nature. Neither his divine nor human generation can be sufficiently praised or adequately represented in words.

---

1) Wittenberg, 1655-77.

2) *Biblia Novi Testamenti illustrata* (3 vols.; Francofurtum, 1676). Annotations to Heb 7:1-10 in III, 1247 ff.

3) The judgment of F.W. Farrar, although overstated, reflects the disputative character of the work. *Biblia* "defends Christianity in the spirit of antichrist, and turns the words of eternal life into an excuse for eternal litigation." *History of Interpretation* (London, 1886), 365.

Other notable representatives or orthodox Lutheran interpretation include Erasmus Schmidt (1570-1637) and Johann
Dorcheus (1597-1659), both of whom make no noteworthy contribution to the understanding of our text. Although a ver-
itable repository of Lutheran interpretation, the exegetical contribution of the latter is swallowed up by extensive
dogmatic and polemic considerations. The copius commentary
of Sebastian Schmidt (1617-96), the Alsace-born dogmatician
and exegete, penetrates rather more deeply into the supposed
meaning of the text.[1] Although manifesting a refreshing absence of polemic, Schmidt's Hebrews commentary betrays a
considerable measure of scholastic dogmatizing, some of
which is little short of fancy.

Schmidt affirms that the terms ἀπάτωρ, ἀμήτωρ, ἀγενεαλόγητος invoke a mystery of no mean proportion. Of no man subsequent to Adam can it be affirmed that he properly lacks
parentage and genealogy. Upon further reflection Schmidt
concedes that even Adam was not fatherless since the Creator
himself stood in a paternal relation to the first man. The
most that can be said of these terms is that by omitting
mention of his parentage and genealogy the Holy Spirit mysteriously ordained that Melchizedek should prefigure Christ
who in a unique and ultimate sense lacks father, mother and
lineage. The dogmatic implications of vs. 3 are far-reaching.
Ἀπάτωρ and ἀμήτωρ, in the first place, refute any notion
of an adoptionist Christology. If Christ had been adopted
by the Father he would be neither "sine patre" nor "sine
matre." Second, the pair affirms that Christ is both true
God and true man. The level of dogmatic pedantry is reflected in Schmidt's attempt to demonstrate the unity and communion of human and divine natures in the one indivisible
Christ. An attempt was made to 'prove' this doctrine by appeal to the typological correspondence between Melchizedek
and Christ. Melchizedek, whom the Holy Spirit designated as
"patrem non habens," "matrem non habens," was clearly a
single person. But since ἀπάτωρ, ἀμήτωρ depict Christ's two
natures, "how much more therefore is Christ, the antitype,

---

1) *Commentarius in epistolam Pauli ad Hebraeos* (Lipsia, 1722[3]), 538 ff.

precisely *one person* with *two natures*."

(c) Reformed Interpretation

Seventeenth century Reformed interpretation experienced
a similar but less pronounced hardening of the theological
arteries than did its Lutheran counterpart. Exegesis was
laden with dogmatic distinctives which solidified into a relatively lifeless orthodox system. Polemic against Roman
Catholic, Socinian and Arminian, although less emotive than
Lutheran disputation, still occupied a prominent place in
Reformed theological literature. A growing interest in the
philology of the biblical text abetted the development of
NT criticism, but this technical advance did little to
rejuvenate what had become rather sterile biblical interpretation. Towards mid-century an interpretive movement led
by Cocceius returned to the Bible itself, which it interpreted by means of a typology which became more extravagant
with the passing of time. The spiritualized exegesis of the
Cocceans was thoroughly rooted in Scripture, but it loaded
the text with manifold nuances elicited from a wide range
of supposed biblical proof texts. Essentially still Christocentric in character, seventeenth century Reformed exegesis nearly lost sight of the type (Melchizedek) in its quest
to extoll the antitype (Christ). Interpreters of the period
experienced particular difficulty explicating the perpetuity
which Hebrews ascribes to Melchizedek in his personal and
official capacities (vss. 3, 8). For this reason not a few
exegetes judged that Melchizedek either had been translated
to heaven in the manner of Enoch or Elijah, or that he was
the Son of God himself in bodily form.

Johannes Piscator (1546-1625), theologian, interpreter
and Bible translator held academic posts in philosophy and
theology at Strasbourg and Heidelberg. The chief exegetical
contribution of this older Reformed interpreter was a copious
Latin commentary on Old and New Testaments.[1] Piscator affirms that vss. 1-3 constitute a preliminary section wherein

---

1) "Analysis logica epistolae Pauli ad Hebraeos," *Commentarii in
omnes libros Novi Testamenti* (Herborna, 1621), 1321 ff.

the historical Melchizedek is set forth as a manifold type
of Christ. Indeed, Piscator's commentary is distinguished
not so much for its penetrating insight into particular exegetical issues, as for its comprehensive grasp of the author's
overall train of thought. The key phrase of the section,
ἀφωμοιωμένος κτλ underscores the Melchizedek-Christ typology.
The six points of correspondence which constitute the symbolic relationship are arranged in two vertical columns.
The statements regarding Melchizedek are realized in the
antitype insofar as the latter is: (i) at once priest and
king; (ii) the king of righteousness who brings his own to
everlasting righteousness; (iii) the true king of peace who
reconciles man with God; (iv) the true priest who has expi-
ated the sins of his people by the sacrifice of himself.
The predicates of vs. 3, based on the silence of the Genesis
record, depict Christ in that the latter is (v) ἀπάτωρ,
ἀμήτωρ as regards his human and divine natures, and (vi) a
priest for eternity because his once for all sacrifice and
continual heavenly intercession are of perpetual efficacy.

In a series of observations on the text Piscator notes
that the Roman Catholic argument concerning Melchizedek's
'offering' of bread and wine in anticipation of the 'sacrifice' of the Mass lacks the authority of Scripture. No more
can be adduced from the Genesis narrative than the fact that
Melchizedek brought forth bread and wine for the physical
refreshment of Abraham's forces. In any event, the doctrine
of the Mass rests on the unproven assumption that during
the Last Supper Christ altered the elements into his body
and blood and that he offered the same to the Father as a
proper sacrifice.

Jacques Cappel III (1570-1624) was a distinguished member of a French family renowned for its long line of eminent
scholars. One of the leading biblical authorities in seventeenth century France, Cappel published in 1624 a series of
learned *observationes* on the NT.[1] While most contemporary
interpreters were engaged in rigid dogmatic and polemical

---

1) *Observationes in Novum Testamentum*, ed. L. Cappel (Amstelodamum,
1657), 170 ff.

expositions of our text, Cappel pioneered critical grammatical and philological research on the NT.

Like most interpreters of the period Cappel affirms that
our text portrays Melchizedek as a type of Christ; however,
the ground upon which the typology is constructed is far
more restrictive than that generally proposed. Cappel limits
the principal similarity between the two priests to the
ascriptions "king of righteousness" and "king of peace."
Reluctant to ascribe eternity to Melchizedek, even in a symbolic sense, the predicates of vs. 3 may properly be applied
only to Christ. Thus preoccupied with Christological concerns of his own age rather than with patriarchial issues,
the apostle affirmed the humanity of Christ by the term
ἀπάτωρ and the divinity of Christ by the expression ἀμήτωρ,
ἀγενεαλόγητος . . . μήτε ζωῆς τέλος ἔχων. When pressed Cappel might concede that μήτε ἀρχὴν ἡμερῶν κτλ teaches that
in contrast to the "principal men of the church" Melchizedek
had no successors in office. Nevertheless the epithets of
vs. 3 apply primarily to Christ.

Cappel is also unwilling to concede that μένει ἱερεὺς
εἰς τὸ διηνεκές characterizes Melchizedek. He allows that
one might attribute a perpetual priesthood to the latter in
much the same way that Hebrews portrays Isaac as one raised
up from the dead ἐν παραβολῇ.[1] But there is no need to postulate the eternity of Melchizedek in order that he might
be a proper type of the Son of God; his royal and priestly
status had already established his typological relationship
to Christ. Hence μένει ἱερεὺς κτλ, in the final analysis,
is descriptive of the antitype alone. An attempt is made to
substantiate this conclusion by inserting a parenthetic
"inquam" and the relative "qui" in the text to yield the
following sense: "Melchizedek, I say, is similar to the Son
of God who remains a priest for ever."

The same attempt to explain away Melchizedek's perpetuity
in priesthood is found in his exegesis of vs. 8. Cappel's
expanded translation of the verse also reveals a unique if
not misplaced geographical emphasis: "Here (in the land of

---

1) Heb 11:19.

Jerusalem where you Hebrews are) dying men receive tithes,
but there (in the land of *Salem*) one receives tithes whose
death is not mentioned in Scripture because he properly
lives." Reluctant to depart from the historical sense and
engage in mystical exegesis by attributing perpetuity to a
mortal figure, Cappel argues that the subject of ζῇ

> is Christ, not because Melchizedek himself would be
> Christ, but because in the person of Melchizedek Christ
> tithed Abraham. Scripture adduces abundant evidence
> that Christ would be alive antonomastically; indeed,
> as the true and living God, he is life itself.

Daniel Heinsius (1580-1655) was one of the eminent scholars of the Dutch Renaissance. The chief exegetical contribution of the Leyden classicist was a learned but on the
whole abstract philological analysis of isolated passages
of the NT.[1] Heinsius' interpretation, which is limited to
detailed notes on vss. 3 and 8, explores the relationship
between these two texts. The view that vs. 8 merely reiterates the teaching of vs. 3 in respect of Melchizedek is
rejected because ὅτι ζῇ is based upon the express declaration of Scripture, whereas the earlier text is constructed
from the mysterious silence thereof. The preferred interpretation is that ὅτι ζῇ refers to "another priest" who
arises after the pattern of Melchizedek (vs. 15), of whom
the Scripture clearly affirms that he bears within himself
"the power of an indestructible life" (vs. 16) and that he
"always lives" (vs. 25). Both ὅτι ζῇ and the primitive declarations of life recorded in the latter half of Hebrews 7
are based upon the testimony of Psa 110:4 ("You are a priest
for ever . . .") and thus refer to none other than the Son
of God himself. Who could suppose, Heinsius reasons, that
the words, "You are a priest for ever" pertain to Melchizedek any more than the command, "Sit at my right hand."

John Cameron (1579-1625), the Scottish-born classicist
and theologian, was associated with the School of Saumur,
which modified traditional Reformed theology by extending
the efficacy of Christ's death to all who exercise faith.
Cameron's earlier interpretive work, prepared from academic

---

1) *Exercitationes sacrae ad Novum Testamentum* (Lugdunum Batavorum,
1639), 564 ff.

lectures delivered at Saumur, was presented in the form of
responses to questions based on select exegetical problems.[1]
The subject matter of this work was only slightly revised
in his other contribution, entitled *Myrothecium evangelicum*.[2]
Both Cameron's NT works display a thorough knowledge of the
biblical languages and generous insight into the exegetical
issues of the text.

"Who was Melchizedek?" In reply to this question Cameron
notes that those who enquire into such a matter pursue an
issue which God himself is unprepared to disclose. For if
the identity of this historical figure were revealed he
would cease to qualify as a proper type of Christ, where-
upon the eternal purpose of God would be frustrated. Hence
contrary to its usual delineation of the life-data of eminent figures of antiquity, Scripture has intentionally concealed the lineage, birth and decease of this anonymous
historical personality that he might foreshadow Christ the
eternal priest. In response to the question, "In what ways
was Melchizedek a type of Christ?" Cameron deviates from
traditional Protestant and Roman Catholic interpretation by
affirming that the symbolic statements of vs. 3 refer not
to the person of Melchizedek (and hence to Christ) but solely
to his priesthood. This is clear since

> Christ had a father in respect of his divinity and a
> mother in respect of his humanity and his genealogy is
> described by Matthew and Luke. In addition, he had a
> beginning of days when he was conceived by the Holy
> Spirit and an end of life when he expired on the cross.

Ἀπάτωρ, ἀμήτωρ, ἀγενεαλόγητος affirm that Melchizedek was
descended from non-priestly ancestry, "that we might not
require in Christ a carnal genealogy as in the case of the
legal priests." Absence of beginning and end of priestly
life, symbolic in the type and real in the antitype, ensures
that the non-Aaronic order of priesthood is totally unique.

During the first half of the seventeenth century when
Reformed and Lutheran interpretation sank to a new low of

---

1) "Ad quaestiones in epistolam Hebraeos," *Praelectiones in selectoria
quaedam NT loca* (3 vols.; Salmurum, 1626-28), III, 243 ff.

2) *Myrothecium evangelicum, in quo aliquot loca NT explicantur* (Geneva, 1632), 322 ff.

sterile orthodoxy, exegesis became the handmaiden of confessional dogmatics and a platform for polemic against op-
posing ecclesiastical parties. Moreover, the message of
Scripture became obscured by learned but abstract philological and historical investigations. Reacting against the
increasing sterility of biblical science, a party of Reformed theologians in Holland in mid-century returned to
Scripture itself with a view to recapturing its living message. The system of federal theology propounded by the party acknowledged an evolutionary progression in divine revelation, wherein OT personalities, institutions and historical eras foreshadowed higher realities in the NT. As a
result, exegesis inherited not only a typology which became
more extravagant with the development of the movement, but
also a hermeneutic which conceded that the meaning of a text
is replete with spiritual and mystical nuances.

Johannes Coccoius (1603-1699) held academic chairs at
the universities of Franeker and Leyden. An extremely pro-
lific scholar, he wrote exegetical works on principal books
of the canonical Scriptures[1] as well as major treatises on
biblical theology, dogmatics and ethics. Coccoius' assertion that Christ is the single great theme in both Testaments
is reflected in his statement that the ultimate purpose of
the Melchizedek pericope (Heb 7:1-10) is to "demonstrate
that the priest according to the order of Melchizedek is
the Son of God." Our text is interpreted according to the
presupposition of the organic unity of Old and New Testaments, wherein neither can be rightly understood apart from
the other. The Hebrews text then must be understood in the
light of Melchizedek's divinely ordained ancient prefiguration of Christ. By virtue of his appearance in the OT as one
who was not born in the customary manner and who never succumbed to death, "Melchizedek plays the part of the Son of
God so that Christ himself might be seen and that as a son
twice born, if it were possible that he should be born
twice." Coccoius' occasional indulgence in mystical exegesis

---

1) *Epistola ad Hebraeos: explicatio et veritatis ejus demonstratio*
(Lugdunum Batavorum, 1659), 255 ff.

and use of dubious points of application are illustrated by
his exposition of vs. 3. Melchizedek admirably portrays
Christ, for as one looks back to the time of Abraham it is
evident that Melchizedek bore the appearance of one who was
not the progeny of human parentage. Likewise, the Son of God
when viewed as a contemporary of Abraham may be regarded as
one who had no human ancestry which could be reckoned. Did
not our Lord himself declare, "Before Abraham was, I am"?
The expression μήτε ἀρχὴν ἡμερῶν . . . εἰς τὸ διηνεκές highlights the thoroughgoing Christocentric character of Cocceius
exposition. The text is properly descriptive not of the
Salemite priest-king but of the priest after the order of
Melchizedek. But since such an ascription of eternity and
perpetuity in office agrees with none save the Son of God,
it follows that the priest "after the order of Melchizedek"
must be Christ himself.

A student of Cocceius at Leyden, Johann Braun (1628-1708)
developed more fully the typological and Christological exegesis introduced by his mentor and predecessor. Although
Braun was highly esteemed as a dogmatician and Hebraist
whose commentaries contain a valuable store of theology,
archaeology and antiquities, his interpretation of Scripture
is characterized by occasional flights of fancy as typological considerations were carried to excess. In order to demonstrate beyond a shadow of a doubt that the ancient Jebu-
site king stands forth as a perfect type of Christ, Braun
affirms in his homiletic commentary[1] that the predicates of
vs. 3 describe both the persons and the offices of the two
priestly figures. Thus μήτε ἀρχὴν ἡμερῶν κτλ depicts Melchizedek in that Scripture recalls nothing of his birth and
decease, precisely as if he had never been born and never
died. In addition, it suggests that the Salemite neither
succeeded another nor was he succeeded in priesthood. In
this official sense Melchizedek is to be regarded as the
first and last of his kind of priesthood.

But the factor which supremely establishes Melchizedek
as a type of Christ as immortal is the deduction drawn from

1) *Commentarius in epistolam ad Hebraeos* (Amstelodamum, 1705), 361 ff.

Psa 110:4 that Melchizedek ζῆ (vs. 8). Braun advances three
reasons why the writer affirms that Melchizedek "vivit
hactenus": (i) in his *personal* capacity, no mention is made
in Scripture of his decease; (ii) in his *official* capacity
Melchizedek lives on in the memory of the church as an eternal type of the priesthood and kingship of Christ; and (iii)
ultimately because subsequent to the fulfillment of his
royal and priestly offices on earth Melchizedek was carried
up to paradise similar to the translation of Enoch and Elijah.
Scripture fails to record in so many words Melchizedek's
translation, but since the text clearly affirms that he
"vivit hactenus" dare one deny that he was thus endowed
with heavenly immortality?

The typological exegesis of the school of Cocceius reached
the peak of extravagance in the biblical exposition of the
Dutch preacher Johann d'Outrein (1662-1722). The fruit of
twenty years preaching on Hebrews, d'Outrein's commentary
is extremely discursive and prolix: the two-volume German
edition[1] fills more than 3,000 quarto pages. Melchizedek
was not merely an exquisite type of Christ (so Braun) or
one who "played the part of the Son of God" (so Cocceius);
rather the ancient Salemite is judged to have been the Son
of God himself clothed in human form, whose appearance in
the primitive history gave antecedent expression to the
priesthood he would formally undertake at his later manifestation. In its straightforward literal sense vs. 3--which
befits the eternal Godhead alone--offers compelling proof
that the Salemite priest-king was a preincarnate manifestation of the Logos. Thus ἀπάτωρ, κτλ affirms that the physical body in which the Son of God met Abraham was "without
father, without mother and was not begotten via ordinary
procreation, but was brought into being directly by God
himself." Nevertheless, d'Outrein is not unaware that the
statement that Melchizedek "resembles" the Son of God tends
to undermine the Christophany thesis: ie, "simile non est
idem." Yet d'Outrein argues from classical philology that

---

1) *Der Brief an die Hebräer* (4 pts. in 2 vols.; Frankfurt & Leipzig,
1713-18), I, ii, 212 ff.

ἀπό in compound strengthens the force of a word. Thus the prefix ἀπό emphasizes the perfection of likeness which exists between the two figures.

> When the apostle employed the word ἀφωμοιωμένος, he wished to declare that both the personal characteristics and the features affirmed of Melchizedek perfectly agree with those attributed to Christ in the gospel. Thus Melchizedek would be the eternal king and priest, that is, Christ himself. Who can be perfectly compared with the Son of God save the Son of God himself? (Psa 89:6; Deut 33:26)

Lest the reader judge that the preceding argument amounts to a *reductio ad absurdum*, d'Outrein suggests that one may legitimately be compared with himself from the standpoint of various personal circumstances: ie, before and after conversion, or in youth vs. maturity. Thus although one's personal identity remains unaltered, there is a sense in which he whose life is compared at different stages may declare, *"ego non sum ego."*

(d) Arminian Paraphrases

The close of the sixteenth century witnessed the rise of Arminian theology which was a reaction to and protest against orthodox, confessional Calvinism. In the main the Arminians adopted a stance independent of the main stream of Protestant and Catholic interpretation, often finding more common ground with contemporary rationalistic movements, particularly Socinianism. The Arminians sought to interpret Scripture impartially on the basis of historical, philological and grammatical considerations alone. Where they approximated the goal of a non-creedal exegesis agreeable to reason, their explication of Scripture was deficient in religious and theological intuition. The Arminian rationalists exercised an incalculable effect upon later interpretation, not only on the Continent but also in England where it proved to be a powerful stimulus to latitudinarian theology.

Jurist, statesman, historian and theologian, Hugo Grotius (1583-1645) was one of the most versatile personalities in seventeenth century Europe. Dissatisfied with the doctrinal rigidity of strict Calvinism, the most influential disciple of James Arminius encountered firm political and ecclesias-

tical opposition in his native Holland. During his lifelong
exile from the Netherlands Grotius wrote widely in his several fields of interest. His annotations on Old and New
Testaments[1] are less a continuous commentary than a historical and philological investigation of select words and
phrases. The *annotationes* set forth a variety of 'parallels'
from classical and Hebrew literature which purport to explicate the meaning of words and phrases of the biblical
text. Grotius' presuppositions about man, nature and revelation are reflected in his exegetical results which evince
an individualistic and rationalistic flavor.

Grotius' emphasis upon the historical side of exegesis
led him to pose the question: "Who was Melchizedek?" Guidance to the problem is found in a treatise of the ancient
Phoenician Sanchuniathon (XIII/XIV BC) who wrote on the
procreation of the deities, the generation of the universe
and the origins of civilization. Grotius supposes that Melchizedek was the astral deity who in the Phoenician treatise
bears the name *Sydyc*. Although scholars question the latter's
existence, the writer of Hebrews discovered in this ancient
mythical figure a model of the NT high priest.

> In the name of this king and priest is concealed a
> mystery which refers in a particular sense to Christ.
> For the latter is a king who administers the most
> perfect justice and the community ("civitas") which
> he has founded both enjoys peace with God and seeks
> peace with all men.

The perpetuity of Melchizedek's ministration is explained
on the assumption that he continued in priesthood "as long
as the cult of the true god continued in Phoenicia." The
figure from Phoenician mythology thus highlights leading
features of the NT priest to come: ie, a ministrant whose
parentage, birth and death are nowhere recorded.

In contrast to traditional Reformed and Lutheran interpretation, Grotius is reluctant to deduce from vs. 3 ontological statements about Christ; Melchizedek is merely a
nonlegal priest-king who exercises an interrupted ministration as long as need exists. Having borrowed extensively

---

1) "Annotationes in epistolam ad Hebraeos," in *opera omnia theologica*
(3 vols.; Amstelodamum, 1679), II, 1031 ff.

from Socinian interpretation, Grotius the generalist made
little independent penetration into the meaning of our text.
Hence there may be a shred of truth in E.G. Robinson's dic-
tum, that "it is ordained of Almighty God that the man who
dips into everything never gets to the bottom of anything."

Educated at Magdalen College, Oxford, Henry Hammond (1605-
60) was a tower of seventeenth century theological science.
A copius writer as well as a highly esteemed preacher, Hammond wrote nearly sixty biblical and theological treatises.
His most distinguished contribution to biblical interpretation was an annotated paraphrase of the NT,[1] the worth of
which is attested by the eight editions through which it
passed. Hammond's *Paraphrase* was made available to the scholarly world at large through the Latin translation of Jean
Le Clerc (1689), who commended the work as being one of the
forerunners of English biblical criticism.

Hebrews' mystical interpretation of the priesthood of
Melchizedek was stimulated by heretical Gnostic interpretations of the OT, which threatened to precipitate the declen-
sion of his readers from faith in Christ. As a corrective,
the writer expounded the "mystical divinity concerning Melchizedek's priesthood." Hammond's interpretation clearly
reflects the influence of Grotius. In respect of his genealogy and pedigree (vs. 3), Melchizedek is portrayed in the
Genesis pericope as the priestly representative of a totally
different race than the Aaronites. The Salemite embodies
the features of an immortal priest since he had neither
predecessor nor successor in office. This unique phenomenon
was due to the fact that Melchizedek was "the last priest
of the true God that was in Phoenicia, idolatry presently
coming in." Unlike traditional orthodox interpretation, the
focus of Hammond's attention is clearly Melchizedek rather
than Christ. The most that can be affirmed about the latter
is that he is a nonlegal priest-king who exercises an uninterrupted ministration as long as need exists.

A further example of the Arminian reaction to creedal

---

1) *A Paraphrase and Annotations Upon all the Books of the New Testament* (London, 1675[4]), 740 ff.

Calvinism and particularly to the elaborate typology of the
school of Cocceius is the French biblical scholar Jean Le
Clerc (1657-1736), who imbibed Socinian notions while a
student. After his open breach with the Calvinists, Le Clerc
was introduced to the Dutch Arminian community by Philip
Limborch, after which he became professor of philosophy,
classics and Hebrew at the Remonstrant Seminary in Amsterdam. The French scholar wrote widely in his chosen disciplines, publishing more than seventy theological works. His
principal contribution to NT interpretation was a Latin
translation of Hammond's *Paraphrase and Annotations* to which
were annexed his own critical and exegetical observations on
selected words and phrases of the Greek text.[1] His own notations were themselves translated into English a year after
publication.[2]

Insisting on the primacy of reason in the deduction of
religious truth, Le Clerc argues that ἀπάτωρ, κτλ signifies
only that the names and accomplishments of Melchizedek's
ancestors had been forgotten with the passing of time. On
the basis of a critical analysis of the Genesis pericope,
Le Clerc deems it highly unlikely that Melchizedek was ordained to serve as an image of Christ either in respect of
his person (absence of parentage, birth and decease) or his
priesthood (lacking predecessor and successor, bearer of an
eternal ministration). On the contrary, guided by an old
Jewish superstition that the Messiah ought to resemble Melchizedek, the writer fashioned an allegorical *ad hominem* argument to show that Christ's priesthood was more noble than
that of Levi. Le Clerc concludes with the hermeneutical observation: "the figurative exposition developed by the author of Hebrews ought not to be encouraged at the present
time, because such a method of explaining Scripture has fal-
len out of currency."

---

1) "Epistola Pauli Apostoli ad Hebraeos," in *Novum Testamentum domini
nostri Jesu Christi* (2 vols.; Amstelodamum, 1698), II, 322 ff.
2) *A Supplement to Dr. Hammond's Paraphrase and Annotations on the
New Testament* (London, 1699).

(e) Puritan Expositors

Radical in theology, fervent in piety and stringent in
ethics, the Puritan divines commanded a degree of influence
on seventeenth century English religious and political life
out of proportion to their numerical strength. By virtue of
their emphasis upon the authority of Scripture, biblical exposition assumed a prominent role in the Puritan economy,
the pulpit being regarded as the most effective channel for
disseminating divine truth. The "doctor" or teaching minister, who was charged with expounding sound doctrine in accord with the biblical mandate, "give attendance . . . to
doctrine,"[1] gave way to the Puritan lectureship which was
supported by powerful gentry patrono. By the middle of the
seventeenth century, scores of Puritan divines were deliv-
ering lectures on biblical and theological themes from prominent city pulpits. The exegetical homilies of the Puritans
were doctrinal, practical, uncritical and generally highly
copious.

William Gouge (1578-1653) was reader in philosophy and
logic at Cambridge before his appointment as rector and lec-
turer at the London church of St. Anne Blackfriars where he
commanded a large following. One of the foremost preachers
of Jacobean England, he served the Blackfriars church for
forty-five years and was popularly acclaimed "the father of
London ministers."[2] Gouge's copious two-volume commentary
on Hebrews[3] is a compilation of 1,000 sermons delivered at
the Blackfriars church during the course of thirty years
"Wednesday's Lectures." His enunciation of the purpose and
scope of Hebrews in "The Proem" demonstrates not only the
vitriolic character of the Puritan polemic, but also something of its idealism and naivete.

> Hebrews may be termed the maul of Popery, which is a
> mass of heresies. Papish heresies are most against
> the offices of Christ, especially against his priest-

---

1) I Tim 4:13.

2) Daniel Neal, *History of the Puritans* (2 vols.; London, 1811), II,
366.

3) *A Learned and Very Useful Commentary on the Whole Epistle to the
Hebrews* (2 vols.; London, 1655), I, ii, 135 ff.

hood. Those heresies are so fully met withall in this
Epistle, as if it had been written since Popery began:
God foreseeing what poisonous heresies would be broached,
prepared this antidote against them.

Gouge maintains that Melchizedek was a proper historical
personage and accepts the common Jewish opinion that Melchizedek was Shem. Unconscious of any dissonance between this
opinion and vs. 3, he adds that the Holy Ghost purposefully
concealed mention of his kindred, birth and decease in order
to affirm orthodox doctrine about Christ. Positively, ἀπάτωρ,
ἀμήτωρ offer compelling support for the hypostatic union of
Christ's human and divine natures. Negatively, the mysteries
inherent in vs. 3 refute most of the ancient Christological
heresies which have assailed the Church. Among these may be
mentioned: the fallacies of the *Proclianites* and *Cerdonians*
(Christ came not in human flesh), the *Manichees* (Christ came
in a feigned species of flesh), the *Valentinians* (Christ
came with a spiritual or celestial body), the *Apollinarists*
(Christ took a soulless flesh), the *Arians* (Christ was a
created being with a certain beginning), the *Ubiquitarians*
(Christ's humanity was endowed with perfect omnipresence),
and the *Samosatenians* (Christ's personal existence commenced
with his incarnation). Clearly Gouge's interpretation is
dominated by profound dogmatic interests.

George Lawson (d. 1678),[1] rector of More, Shropshire, focused attention upon the three principal figures in Hebrews
7: Melchizedek (priest according to the law of Nature), Aaron
(priest according to the law of Moses), and Christ (priest
according to the law of Grace). The first, Melchizedek, adumbrates the last, Christ, in a threefold manner: (i) in
offices (the union of priesthood and kingship), (ii) in acts
or deeds (the reception of tithes and the blessing), and
(iii) in the continuance of his priesthood. Whereas the all
important final point might be established by recalling that
the priesthood of Melchizedek, like that of Christ, was not
transmitted to any successor, the argument for perpetuity
becomes "more fully and lively" if we allow that "Melchizedek's sacerdotal title did . . . continue to him in heaven

---

1) *An Exposition of the Epistle to the Hebrews* (London, 1662), 94 ff.

until Christ's ascension, and then was delivered up to Christ, and so it continued in him for ever." Surely a ministrant translated to heaven in a state of life (ὅτι ζῆ) would merit the affirmation, "he abideth a priest continually."

Norton Knatchbull (1602-85)[1] advances an interpretation of Heb 7:1 ff. which we have not encountered heretofore. Οὗτος (vs. 1) is related not to Μελχισέδεκ which follows, but to 'Ιησοῦς which immediately precedes (ch. 6:20). Moreover, the lengthy expression ὁ Μελχισέδεκ . . . τῷ υἱῷ τοῦ θεοῦ is to be enclosed within parentheses and set in apposition to 'Ιησοῦς, to yield the following interpretation:

> For this Jesus, who is entered into the inner part of the veil, etc. (ch. 6:19, 20), being the Melchizedek . . . , that is, prefigured in Melchizedek, who was like unto him in that he is called the priest of the most high God, king of righteousness and peace, having neither beginning of days nor end of life, attributes congruous only to the Son of God; I say, this *Jesus*, according to the true and genuine interpretation of the words, abideth a priest continually, but not Melchizedek.

Knatchbull insists that this preferred alternative construction safely avoids two flagrant contradictions inherent in traditional interpretations: "the one in *nature*, that a mortal man should live for ever, and the other in *faith*, that there should be two high priests that should live for ever."

Similarly vs. 8: since Scripture nowhere ascribes immortality to Melchizedek, ὅτι ζῆ can only apply to Jesus the Son of God (cf. vss. 24, 25). Thus the text reads: "ὧδε-- here in this world--tithes are received by mortal men; ἐκεῖ --there in heaven--by Christ of whom it is testified that he lives." Knatchbull's thesis that "Jesus is the true Melchizedek" enables him to avoid the patent absurdity that the heavenly Christ received tithes from the patriarch.

John Owen (1616-83) is unquestionably the foremost Puritan expositor of Hebrews. The nominal head of English Congregationalism during the regime of Oliver Cromwell, Owen held influential posts both within the church and in politics. His most celebrated contribution to biblical inter-

---

1) *Animadversiones in libros Novi Testamenti* (Oxford, 1676[3]), 162 ff.

pretation was an exhaustive commentary on Hebrews,[1] which even after 300 years retains considerable popularity and appeal. The massive four-volume folio work reflects a masterful mixture of exegetical observations, doctrine and polemic, but the exposition is also tedious and discursive.

Owen deems the identity of Melchizedek a matter charged with spiritual significance. Although the latter dwelt in the land of Canaan, under no circumstance could he be numbered amongst the progeny of Ham upon whom God's curse rested. Rather, Melchizedek was a descendant of Japheth, the progenitor of the great company of Gentiles whom God would summon to constitute his Church. The covenant blessing was pronounced upon Shem in anticipation of the promised Seed who would emerge from his posterity.[2] But before this promise was brought to fruition and in accord with the divine counsel,

> God brought this Melchizedek and other posterity of Japheth into the land of Canaan, even before Abraham . . . had possession of it, and placed him there in a condition of office superior unto Abraham himself: that he might manifest that the state of Gentile converts . . . should be far more excellent and better than was the state and privileges of the posterity of Shem whilst in their separate condition, God having provided some better things for us that they without us should not be made perfect.

Owen's exegesis of the text, which reflects similarities to the Reformed school of Cocceius, is on the whole responsible and restrained. At first sight the epithets of vs. 3 appear "strange and uncouth." But understood in the light of the silence of the OT, the text affords a comprehensive delineation both of Christ's priesthood and of his person. Owen's explication of these mysteries is not entirely free from scholastic encrustations, particularly his explanation of the death of Christ in relation to the typological affirmation that Christ has no ζωῆς τέλος. Argues Owen:

> For although the person of the Son of God died . . . yet he died not in his whole person. . . . So whilst he was dead in the earth in his human nature, the same

---

1) *Exercitations on the Epistle to the Hebrews* (4 vols.; London, 1668-74), III, 89 ff.
2) Gen 9:26.

person was alive in his divine. Absolutely therefore
. . . he had neither beginning of days nor end of life.

3. THE EIGHTEENTH CENTURY

(a) English Paraphrases

By the beginning of the eighteenth century a profusion
of paraphrases and annotations on the NT were being produced.
Traditional commentaries were supplanted by the paraphrastic form for at least two reasons: (i) a desire to liberate
biblical interpretation from the dominance of dogmatic and
polemic interests by allowing the biblical documents to
speak for themselves; and (ii) a growing conviction that the
diffuse commentaries of the seventeenth century should be
replaced by a more succinct interpretive form. Insulated
by geography and temperament from the Continental scene,
British interpreters of the period mirror the theological
debates indigenous to their own soil. Thus commentators found
themselves posited on one side or the other of running theological debates between loyal churchmen and dissenters, between conservative and liberal factions of the Church of
England, or between proponents of traditional orthodoxy and
advocates of Socinianism, Arminianism or Deism. English theologians and exegetes of liberal persuasion subjected the
faith to thorough rational examination in order to demonstrate the primacy of reason over revelation. Antitrinitarian
tendencies, which sought to reduce Christ to the level of
a created being, exercised a determinative influence upon
the interpretation of our text.

Daniel Whitby (1638-1726), a learned NT commentator who
took his degree at Trinity College, Oxford, was a leading
proponent of Arminianism within the Anglican communion. In
later life Whitby's latitudinarian tendencies blossomed
forth into full-grown Unitarianism.[1] Judged by his numerous

---

1) As clearly articulated in *The Last Thoughts of Dr. Whitby* (London,
1828). Whitby asserts in the preface of this work that mature reflection
occasioned a change of fundamental convictions: "When I wrote my commentaries on the NT, I went on (too hastily I own) in the common beaten
road of other reputed orthodox divines; conceiving first, that the Father, Son, and Holy Ghost, in the one complex notion, were one and the
same God, by virtue of the same individual essence communicated from the
Father. This confused notion I am now fully convinced . . . to be a thing
impossible, and full of gross absurdities, and contradictions." (no
pagination)

polemic treatises, Whitby was an active participant in various theological controversies with the Roman Catholic, Socinian and Calvinist parties. The year 1703 marked the publication of his principal exegetical work, a two-volume folio paraphrase with commentary of the NT,[1] which was frequently republished well into the nineteenth century.

In opposition to traditional Roman Catholic and Protestant exegesis, Whitby is reluctant to affirm that the so-called typology of vss. 1-3 elicits truth concerning Christ. Thus no typological correspondence is forged by the epithets "king of righteousness" and "king of peace." The most Whitby is prepared to affirm is that "Melchizedek was in this like unto him (ie, Christ), that he was both a priest of the most High God, and a king also in that country, those two offices being anciently in the same person." Similarly, the expression ἀπάτωρ, ἀμήτωρ, κτλ refers only to Melchizedek, since Christ possessed a mother and his priestly office had a clear point of beginning.[2] Hence the text affirms only that Melchizedek lacked the customary priestly parentage and pedigree and that his ministration had no discernible commencement and termination. Moreover, ἀφωμοιωμένος κτλ establishes no correspondence whatever between Melchizedek and Christ, but merely affirms that the former was "like to a son of God, or to *one of the angels* who are immortal and never cease to be." The contention that υἱός (even with the definite article) denotes an angel is argued by appeal to the fact that "Bene Heloim" is employed in the OT of angelic beings (ἄγγελοι τοῦ θεοῦ, LXX).[3] In terms of the context of vs. 3, it is more logical and consistent that the apostle should have likened Melchizedek to an angel rather than to Christ, since in Hebrews 7 Christ is likened to the priestly order of Melchizedek and not the converse.

James Peirce (1674-1726) served Presbyterian congregations in Britain, rising to prominence as a learned and articulate non-conformist divine. A cursory examination of his writings

---

1) *A Paraphrase and Commentary on the New Testament* (2 vols.; London, 1760[7]), II, 539.
2) Cf. Luke 3:23.
3) Eg, Job 1:6; 2:1. Cf. Job 38:7.

reveals that he held to a Unitarian or, at least, a Sabel-
lian view of Christ. William Whiston, the prominent eighteenth century Arian, described Peirce as "the most learned
of all the dissenting teachers that I have known."[1] Notwith-
standing his erudition, Peirce was discharged from the ministry in 1719 when the antitrinitarian issue came to a head.
His highly regarded commentary on Hebrews[2] was translated
into Latin and emendations added by J.D. Michaelis (1747).
It is reported that after his decease Peirce's tombstone
was to have been inscribed with the epitaph: "Here lies the
reverend, learned and pious Mr. James Peirce." But objection
was tendered by at least one clerical colleague that the
ascription "pious" was wholly inappropriate since Peirce
propagated theological error.[3]

Peirce sought to minimize the Christological implications
of our text by an argument which is entirely novel. No rational interpreter could suppose that as regards his person
Melchizedek had no beginning of life. Likewise, the view
that μήτε ἀρχὴν ἡμερῶν κτλ delineates "days of priestly service" fails to convince, since the beginning of the priesthood of his "parallel" is known to have taken place at his
resurrection. Consistent with a valid classical usage, ἀρχὴν
should be taken in an adverbial sense, with the force of
"prorsus," "plane" or "omnino." Peirce's paraphrase of vs.
3 reads thus: "Melchizedek . . . was without any priestly
descent either by his father's or mother's side, *having not
any end of all his days or life*, but was made like unto the
Son of God, Jesus Christ, who abideth a priest continually."
This result is then applied to the NT priest.

> For this Melchizedek, of the end of the days of whose
> priesthood, or of the end of whose priestly life the
> scripture is wholly silent, will well answer to our
> Lord Jesus Christ, who being once vested in his office,
> is a priest for ever, or after the power of an endless
> life.

A question immediately arises in the mind of the reader.
Since Peirce had already asserted that Melchizedek (and thus

---

1) *DNB*, XV, 681.
2) *A Paraphrase and Notes on the Epistle to the Hebrews* (London, 1727),
117 ff.
3) *DNB*, XV, 684.

Christ) was descended from non-priestly ancestry, why did
he set aside the seemingly agreeable interpretation that
Melchizedek had no beginning of days in priestly service in
favor of a less probable construction which (with the possible exception of Jn 8:25) appears nowhere else in the NT?
Peirce's Christology--particularly the notion that the Son
was begotten by the Father in time--appears to have dictated
the terms of his exegesis and obviated the possibility of
ascribing to Christ a priesthood which was eternal *a parte
ante*. Thus Peirce is guilty of making the biblical text read
as he believes *a priori* it ought to read.

After taking theological degrees at Corpus Christi College, Cambridge, the latitudinarian divine Arthur Ashley
Sykes (1684-1756) served parish churches in various parts
of England. His paraphrastic commentary on Hebrews[1] evinces
many of the emphases enunciated by classical Socinian interpretation. Immunity from the rule of priestly succession is
regarded as the principal teaching of our text concerning
the ancient Salemite priest-king. Thus μήτε ἀρχὴν ἡμερῶν κτλ
contrasts Melchizedek not with the Aaronite priests, but
with the larger tribe of Levi. Since the priestly law required that the Levites be thirty years of age before undertaking the service of the tabernacle and that their duties
be relinquished at fifty years,[2] the Levites were governed
by a fixed schedule of accession and succession to office.
Melchizedek, on the other hand, was not bound by any rule
of succession based on descent, but exercised an uninterrupted priestly ministry. In the same manner, since the Son
of God neither derived his office from a law of tribal succession nor did he succumb to death as a priest, he also
administers a perpetual priesthood. Clearly Sykes avoided
traditional ontological affirmations in respect of the person of Christ. The indifference of the latitudinarian to
dogmatic formulations precluded such a possibility.

---

1) *A Paraphrase and Notes Upon the Epistle to the Hebrews* (London,
1755), 84 ff.
2) Numb 4:3, 35, 39, 43; 8:25.

(b) Antiquarian Investigations

The eighteenth century witnessed heightened interest in disciplines which historically had been either neglected or at most peripheral to biblical exegesis: eg, oriental history, antiquities, archaeology and chronology. This development reflects a clear shift in method from interpretation along narrow scholastic and dogmatic lines to preoccupation with ancient language, literature and customs as vehicles for unfolding the meaning of Scripture. Interpreters in this tradition isolated a corpus of literature roughly contemporary with apostolic Christianity and hailed this body as the key which would unravel once and for all the exegetical problems of the Epistle. Thus the philologist Schöttgen stressed the Jewishness of Hebrews and sought to explicate its meaning by appeal to the traditions of rabbinic Judaism. Carpzov, the classicist, viewed Hebrews through the spectacles of Philo. The Arminian Wettstein, a student of classical literature, interpreted the NT in terms of the Latin and Greek classics. Although many interpreters who pursued such research were adherents of confessional orthodoxy, confirmation of doctrine was sought on philological and historical rather than on dogmatic grounds.

Christian Schöttgen (1687-1751), who developed a lifelong interest in Oriental languages, literature and philology, devoted himself to the interpretation of the NT in the light of the corpus of rabbinic literature. Schöttgen's celebrated work--*Horae Hebraicae*[10]--was intended to supplement and extend the research into the Jewish background of the NT undertaken seventy-five years earlier by John Lightfoot, the English rabbinic scholar.

In the preface to his work Schöttgen laments the fact that interpreters continue to tread the well-worn path of attempting to illuminate the NT by appeal to the writings of profane Gentile authors. Since the ancient Greeks were "a perverse and godless people" estranged from divine reve-

---

1) *Horae Hebraicae et Talmudicae* (2 vols.; Dresda & Lipsia, 1733-42), I, 958 ff.

lation, their writings are the least likely source of useful literary parallels. Hence Schöttgen urges the serious student of the NT "to return to the Jews, to the fellow-citizens and blood relations of Christ and the apostles, who inform us of many more matters than all the Gentile authors."[1] The thesis of Schöttgen's work, therefore, is that the voluminous rabbinic writings accurately reflect the traditions of first century Judaism and hence diffuse immeasurable light on the apostolic writings which were rooted, after all, in Jewish not Gentile soil. However, Schöttgen's occasional admission of frivolous interpretations of the later rabbis was indiscriminate and his exaltation of rabbinic theology was unduly idealistic.[2]

The triad ἀπάτωρ, ἀμήτωρ, ἀγενεαλόγητος (vs. 3) is the subject of an extended investigation. Melchizedek's representation as a figure who was devoid of father, mother and genealogy are to be understood in the light of the biblical prescriptions whereby the legal priest was required (i) to verify from the Jewish genealogies legitimate descent from the family of Aaron,[3] and (ii) to marry a virgin--not a widow, nor her that was divorced, nor a harlot--from among the Jewish race.[4] The rabbis judged a man ἀπάτωρ and thus unfit for priestly service who was the son of a proselyte, a slave, a prisoner of war, or whose father practiced a base profession. The Talmud records the example of Alexander

---

1) "Praefatio," I, par. iv. To the objection of critics who argued that scarcely any reliable doctrine could be deduced from those who thoroughly abused the Messiah, Schöttgen replies that not all the Jews acted thus; some were converted and others subscribed to a thoroughly orthodox theology.

2) In the "Praefatio" Schöttgen argues that the Jewish doctrine of the Messiah confounds the doctrines of "the *Priests*, who snatch a great part of his glory to themselves; the *Socinians*, for whom Messianic ideas are virtually non-existent; the *Deists*, so-called, and other men in England of licentious and fanatical spirit who affirm that Jesus was deceitful and who cast doubt upon his miracles and resurrection. It confounds all those who twist the sacred texts about the Messiah into another sense. All those are thrown into disgrace by the Jews who certainly handled the relevant texts far more accurately and who displayed greater love toward the Messiah than those who were born and brought up in the bosom of the Christian church and who pride themselves with the name Christians."

3) Lev 21:10. Cf. Ezra 2:62; Neh 7:64.

4) Lev 21:13 ff.

Jannaeus who was petitioned to divest himself of high priestly functions because his mother had been a captive.[1] Schöttgen
concludes from the foregoing strands of thought that ἀπάτωρ,
κτλ describes the lowly estate of the Gentiles since their
family heads are not enumerated in the Jewish registers.[2]
Suidas, the Greek lexicographical work, supports this position: Melchizedek was portrayed by Moses as lacking parentage and genealogy because he was a Gentile--indeed, because
he was descended from the accursed seed of the Canaanites--
and thus was deemed unworthy of mention in the ancestral
registers of the Jews. Thus it follows that Melchizedek's
antitype is superior to the legal priests since his family
register required no scrutiny whatsoever.

> The first superiority of Christ is this: there was no
> need that his family be subjected to the rigorous exam-
> ination of others, to which the rest of the priests were
> required to subject themselves. In this respect he was
> similar to Melchizedek.

Johann Benedikt Carpzov (1720-1803) was one of the last
significant representatives of the old school of Lutheran
orthodoxy. The principal hermeneutical presupposition which
governs his Hebrews commentary[3] is the conviction that obscure words, enigmatic figures of speech and elusive concepts are clarified when compared with the writings of Philo.
Carpzov judges that Hebrews' linguistic and conceptual af-
finities with Philo were a matter of divine design since the
Alexandrian stood closer to the language and thought milieu
of the evangelists and apostles than any other extra-biblical writer. Constructing an elaborate system of Philonic
dependence initiated earlier by the researches of Hugo Grotius
and Thomas Mangey (editor of Philo), Carpzov unfolds the
meaning of the text by appeal to numerous 'parallels' from
the writings of the Alexandrian philosopher. Ironically, by
virtue of his preoccupation with the Philonic genre of He-

---

1) b. Kidd. 66.a.
2) Bereshith R. XVIII.5 is cited: "If a man became a proselyte, and
he was (previously) married to his paternal sister or to his maternal
sister, he must in rabbi Meir's opinion divorce her. But the sages maintain: he must divorce his maternal sister, but he may keep his paternal
sister, for a Gentile does not have a father."
3) *Sacrae exercitationes in S. Paulli epistolam ad Hebraeos ex Philone
Alexandrino* (Helmstadium, 1750), 293 ff.

brews, the staunch defender of Lutheran orthodoxy laid bare
the Hellenistic character of the Epistle which, unbeknown
to him, would be carried to further extremes by the eighteenth century Tübingen school and the later history of religions movement.

Carpzov advocated a literal, non-allegorical understanding
of the Genesis 14 account, in which Melchizedek is regarded
as a distinguished Canaanite priest-king committed to the
maintenance of the true religion. The distinctive features
of Melchizedek's life and priesthood were purposefully inserted in the Genesis narrative in order to represent him
as a figure and type of the Messiah. The phrase μήτε ἀρχὴν
ἡμερῶν κτλ demonstrates the thoroughgoing influence of Philo
upon his exegesis. Carpzov is attracted to Philo's representation of Noah as the one whom God deemed "worthy to be
both the *last* (τέλος) and the *first* (ἀρχή) of our kind--
last of those who lived before the flood and first of those
who lived after it."[1] Having thus discovered the Philonic
key which unlocks the meaning of the phrase, Carpzov renders
the expression: "qui primus est atque ultimus in sui generis
sacerdotio." Melchizedek's uniqueness resides in the fact
that his priestly ministration was not restricted to particular days, sabbaths, or festivals prescribed by the law.

Textual critic and interpreter of the NT, Johann Jacob
Wettstein (1673-1754) developed a lifelong interest in the
variant readings of the received text, an endeavor which
incited the displeasure of orthodox colleagues in the Swiss
Reformed Church. Dismissed from pastoral and academic posts
in Basel, Wettstein found the climate of the Dutch Remon-
strants more suitable for his text-critical labors. In his
annotated Greek text of the NT,[2] Wettstein sought to elucidate the meaning of key words and phrases guided by the principle that the NT must be interpreted as any other literary
document.

By way of illustrating the words ἀπάτωρ, ἀμήτωρ Wettstein
cites from the *Onomasticon* of Pollux (III.26), wherein Athena

---

1) *De Abr.* 46.
2) *Η ΚΑΙΝΗ ΔΙΑΘΗΚΗ* (2 vols.; Amstelodamum, 1751-52), II, 407 ff.

is designated ἀμήτωρ by virtue of the fact that when the
head of Zeus was severed by an axe, the goddess emerged into
life. Likewise Hephaestus (the god of the smithy fire) is
denoted ἀπάτωρ since he was begotten by Hera alone, who subsequently cast her offspring out of heaven when it became
apparent that he was deformed. Yet Wettstein also directs
attention to citations from Eusebius[1] and Josephus[2] where
the pair relate to absence of parentage in the Levitical
genealogies. In any case, the argument of vs. 3 is regarded
as an allegorical exposition akin to that devised by the
Jewish rabbis.

(c) Pietistic Exposition

Seventeenth century pietism was a separatistic movement
in reaction to formalistic, creedal orthodoxy on one hand,
and rationalistic tendencies in religion on the other. P.J.
Spener (d. 1705) is regarded as the founding father of the
movement which produced other celebrated theologians such
as A.H. Francke (d. 1727) and J. Lange (d. 1744). The pietists sought to recapture the Reformation emphasis of a
practical and personal religion based on the authority of
Scripture. By insisting that spiritual edification, subjective experience and practical piety constitute the kernel
of true religion, the pietists frequently dismissed theological scholarship as irrelevant. In lieu of scientific investigations, pietistic interpreters plumbed the depths of
Scripture to extract multiple and mystical meanings which
abetted the religious edification of the reader. Whereas
Halle pietism became increasingly introspective and by the
middle of the eighteenth century was in a state of recession,
pietism in Württemberg flourished under the genius of J.A.
Bengel, who insisted that both sound scholarship and authentic religious experience are indispensable requirements of
the theologian.

Johann Jakob Rambach (1693-1737), whose Hebrews commen-

---

1) *H.E.* 1.3.
2) *Ant.* XI.3.10.

tary is based on university lectures on the Epistle,[1] insisted that since God is the author of Holy Writ the task
of the interpreter is to extract from the biblical text as
much fullness of meaning as the words will sustain. The rule
of thumb one follows is the *analogia fidei*, by which the
exegete unfolds the meaning of divine revelation in proportion to the strength and clarity of his faith. Indeed, the
multiple sense of a text is to be admitted if the several
senses are in harmony with the teaching of Scripture as a
whole.

Rambach's explication of our text reveals two features
of his exegesis: (i) the statements regarding the Canaanitic
type (especially vss. 2, 3 and 8) take on ultimate meaning
only when applied to Christ, and (ii) a *fullness* if not a
plurality of meaning is ascribed to the text. The word
ἀγενεαλόγητος teaches that on the human side Jesus had no
generic link with the disenfranchised tribe of Levi. But
lest any interpretive stone be left unturned, Christ is devoid of genealogical register not only in respect of his
humanity but also in respect of his *divinity*. This is so on
the following account: "For although he is a distinct person from the Father, yet the *essentia Patris* is not multi-
plied in him, since he is one reality with the Father."

Johann Albrecht Bengel (1687-1752) embodied the noblest
ideals of German pietism. The title of his dedicatory speech
at the Denkendorf seminary, where he served for nearly three
decades, highlights the principle which characterized his
life's work: "The diligent pursuit of piety is the surest
method of attaining sound learning."[2] Bengel's *opus magnum*,
the fruit of twenty year's labor, is his celebrated *Gnomon*
of the NT.[3] The subtitle of the work reflects its innate
genius: *Gnomon* was intended to point out "the natural force
of the words, the simplicity, depth, consistency and saving
power of the divine revelation." Since Scripture is its own

---

1) *Gründliche und erbauliche Erklärung der Epistel Pauli an die
Hebräer* (Frankfurt & Leipzig, 1742), 239 ff.
2) J.C.F. Burk, *A Memoir of the Life and Writings of J.A. Bengel*
(London, 1837), 35.
3) *Gnomon Novi Testamenti* (Tubinga, 1773[3]), 1088 ff.

interpreter, *Gnomon* was to be a helpful "pointer" or "index"
to the truth of the biblical revelation.[1] Bengel's exegetical
annotations reflect a brilliant union embracing profound insight into the letter of the biblical text together with
animated morsels of religious and spiritual truth which e-
volve from the letter.

While advancing no radically new interpretation of our
text, Bengel here and there offers a fresh emphasis worthy
of note. The operative word in the expression μήτε ἀρχήν
ἡμερῶν κτλ is the verb ἔχων, the implicit basis of the statement being "with Moses." Although recording the death of the
Aaronic priests, Moses mysteriously omitted mention of Melchizedek's birth and decease thus intimating the eternity
of the Son of God. Bengel observes that it would have been
unsuitable for the apostle to have utilized the customary
expression, "the beginning of life," or "the end of days,"
because in vs. 16 "life" is associated with "power." In its
entirety, vs. 3 "holds good in the strict sense from Christ."

(d) Transitional Theology

Here interpreters adopted a mediating stand between traditional dogmatic and confessional theology, on one hand,
and new rationalistic tendencies on the other. The roots of
the transitional theologians arose out of orthodoxy and pietism, but they later assimilated rationalistic emphases
from the eighteenth century theological Enlightenment. Reason rises to the fore to challenge revelation as the primary
means of discerning religious truth, and philosophical concepts traditionally subservient to theology gain wider currency. In reaction to the dogmatic exegesis of the previous
century, transitional theologians displayed increasing indifference to dogma and creedal formulae. Similar tendencies
had evolved among the Arminians in Holland during the latter
half of the seventeenth century and in England during the
early decades of the eighteenth. One now witnesses an analogous reorientation of orthodox Lutheran interpretation in

---

1) Cf.: "The Gnomon points the way with sufficient clarity. If you
are wise, the text itself will teach you all things." *Gnomon*, iii.

Germany at the hands of a rising tide of neological currents.

Pastor, hymnologist and biblical scholar Johann Andreas
Cramer (1723-88) held chairs of theology at Copenhagen and
Kiel. Cramer is remembered for some 400 religious poems and
hymns and for a Hebrews commentary[1] which, while giving as-
sent to traditional orthodoxy, also embodies traces of contemporary neology. Cramer thus stood at the fore of a search-
ing reappraisal of traditional exegetical results. It remained for his Lutheran successors to carry the quest to
further lengths and to directly challenge the results of
traditional orthodox interpretation.

Cramer's thesis is that "Melchizedek was ordained by God
not as a *Vorbild* of the God-man, but as a *Vorbild* of Christ
the priest." Interpreters who construct from the text a system of dogma are motivated more by personal prejudice than
by firm evidence. Thus the traditional opinion that ἀπάτωρ,
ἀμήτωρ, ἀγενεαλόγητος signify the humanity, divinity and
eternal generation of Christ is entirely without foundation.
Cramer insists that one must add to the foregoing triad the
phrase ἐξ φυλῆς Λευί.

Similarly challenged is the time-honored thesis that want
of "beginning of days" and "end of life" characterizes the
eternity of the NT priest. On the contrary, μήτε ἀρχὴν ἡμερῶν
implies that Melchizedek's accession to priestly office was
without the solemn week-long ceremonial consecration to which
the Levitical priests were required to undergo, and μήτε
ζωῆς τέλος signifies that the Salemite ministrant was devoid
of priestly successors. Appropriating an earlier observation of Grotius, Cramer argues that "Melchizedek remains a
priest as long as the state of affairs in the church of Canaan permitted."

The early upbringing of the celebrated Göttingen Orientalist Johann David Michaelis (1717-91) was in the tradition of
strict orthodoxy. One of his early essays defended the divine authority of the vowel points of the Hebrew Bible. At
Halle he was greatly influenced by the nascent rationalism

---

1) *Erklärung des Briefes Pauli an die Hebräer* (2 vols.; Kopenhagen
& Leipzig, 1757), II, 79 ff.

of S. J. Baumgarten (1706-57), and his association with the
English Deists in 1741 further contributed to his breach
with orthodoxy. In 1747 Michaelis translated Peirce's *Paraphrase and Notes on Hebrews* into Latin,[1] appending his own
exegetical observations. In his later commentary on Hebrews,[2]
Michaelis altered many earlier views on the basis of newly
acquired critical principles. His ultimate predilection for
rationalistic views did much to hasten the demise of eighteenth century orthodoxy and the rise of a full-fledged theological rationalism.

Michaelis abandoned the typological mode of interpreting
our text and focused attention entirely upon the OT figure
of Melchizedek. As to the latter's identity, Michaelis adopts
an attitude of complete detachment.

> It appears to me that Melchizedek would have been Mel-
> chizedek and the question, who he otherwise would have
> been is as foolish as if I wished to ask Miltiades who
> he otherwise had been. . . . One would not have come
> to such foolishness if he had not presumed to know the
> whole of antiquity so precisely that he could recite
> on his finger the entire genealogy and history of every
> man who appeared on the scene.

The alpha-privative triad ἀπάτωρ, κτλ in no sense appoints
Melchizedek a type of the Messiah. To discern the sense of
the Oriental idiom one must turn to the writings of the Arabs
rather than to the Greek classics. Thus when the Arabs say,
"he has no father," they mean that "he is so eminent that
one completely forgets to mention his father but thinks solely of him and his personal renown."

In view of his depreciation of the Christological implications of the first part of the text Michaelis experiences
no little difficulty with the clause ἀφωμοιωμένος τῷ υἱῷ τοῦ
θεοῦ. Taken at face value the words appear to be an artifi-
cial composition arranged for the purpose of representing
Melchizedek as a figure of the Messiah in respect of sundry
personal or priestly features. But an alternative solution
to the typological construction is proposed by appealing to

---

1) *Peircii paraphrasis et notae philologicae atque exegeticae in
epistolam ad Hebraeos* (Hala, 1747), 264 ff.
2) *Erklärung des Briefes an die Hebräer* (Frankfurt & Leipzig, 1780-
86[2]), 228 ff.

his thesis that the extant Greek text of Hebrews is a translation from a Hebrew original.[1] The primitive Hebrew text
clearly would have lacked an article before "son" which governs a following genitive. Michaelis argues that the definite
article was probably added to the Greek text by the translator for dogmatic reasons. Thus the clause under consideration ought to read: "he (ie, Melchizedek) is similar to *a*
son of God." Hence the apostle "on the basis of the Mosaic
narrative regarded Melchizedek as an *angel* whose father,
mother, family, birth and decease could not be reported."
So marked was Melchizedek's likeness to an angel, that some
early students of Hebrews were persuaded that he really was
an angel in human form!

(e) *Rationalistic Interpretation*

Interpreters in the rationalist tradition were motivated
by the conviction that the traditional faith, smothered by
antiquated, prescientific conceptions and irrelevant dogmas,
must be discarded in favor of a more reasonable and enlightened religion. Thus there emerged in the latter quarter of
the eighteenth century a skeptical movement which not only
challenged the tenets of orthodox theology, but which also
attacked the time-honored sources from which religious truth
is derived. At the outset the rationalists merely sought to
articulate a more reasonable faith. But as the movement developed interpreters discarded the concept of immediate divine revelation and the inspiration of Scripture, in particular, in favor of the exaltation of human reason as the final
authority in religion. Hence the rationalists assumed the
right to reject whatever traditional dogmas proved antithe-
tic to reason and good sense. Since the Hebrew and Christian Scriptures were penned by fallible, biased writers, the
legends and philosophy of the ancients must be held as equally valid sources of religious truth. The rationalists' sim-
plification of religion to a system of responsible morality

---

1) For an explication of the thesis see his *Einleitung in die göttlichen Schriften des Neuen Testaments* (2 vols.; Göttingen, 1788[4]), vol
II, ch. 14, par. ix, xiii.

which guides man to ascending stages of felicity, reduced
the theological body of the Christian religion to little more
than a skeleton.

The critical conjectures of the Halle theologian Johann
Salomo Semler (1725-91) earned him the title, "the father of
German rationalism."[1] Semler held that a line of demarcation
should be drawn between personal religion and formal, scientific theology. Thus whereas he was skeptical of the validity of many dogmas of the church in their current state
of evolution, he nevertheless sought to foster personal piety on the basis of experience and reason. Semler is generally regarded as the first German theologian to have applied
a truly historico-critical methodology to the canon and text
of the Bible. Post-Reformation exegesis was in the main dogmatic, confessional, and in later decades grammatical. But
Semler formulated the thesis that the NT is a diverse historical composition whose constituent parts bears the indel-
ible stamp of the culture and outlook of the people to whom
it was addressed. Hence many of the apostolic teachings em-
body merely local and temporal truths applicable to the circumstances of the first century world. Moreover, since the
OT was directed to the Jewish people and fulfilled a temporary purpose in respect of the Jews, many of its teachings
are of little relevance either to the faith of the early
church or to Christians today.

Semler's paraphrase of vss. 1-3[2] sketches his novel hermeneutical approach to the text.

> One can understand that the religious situation of the
> ancient Jews is of little use to us in the present. Thus
> if you read the account of Melchizedek you find that
> he had no father, mother or relations. Likewise, neither
> the time of his birth nor of this death is announced
> in the record. Moreover, by these means he is repre-
> sented as one like the Son of God and Messiah and there-
> fore his priesthood still continues.

Semler judges that the foregoing Jewish argument is of antiquarian interest only to the modern reader. By appealing

---

1) *EB*, 11th ed., XXIV, 630.
2) "Beiträge zu genauerer Einsicht des Briefes an die Hebräer," in
S.J. Baumgarten's, *Erklärung des Briefes St. Pauli an die Hebräer* (Halle,
1763), 125 ff.

to the Jewish addressees in their particular cultural and
historical circumstances via an argument appropriate to them
alone, the author sought to demonstrate that the Levitical
institution had been superceded by a more eminent priestly
order. In order to so demonstrate Christ's superiority to
Levi, Hebrews consciously appealed to the prevailing Jewish
belief that the one whose parentage and descent is omitted
in Gen 14:18 ff. must be a shadow of the Son of God. Thus
Melchizedek's representation in vs. 3 should be regarded as
no more than an argument derived from the Genesis narrative
by way of concession to the superstitions of first century
Jews who would have readily identified one who lacked birth
and decease with the Son of God. Because Heb 7:1 ff. is an
argumentum e concessu and thus far removed from the reality
of the present situation, Semler insists that the text never
should be taken as a basis for typological statements about
Christ: "We ought not torture ourselves with such forced
propositions which for us are irrelevant and for the Jews
most useless." The most he is willing to concede is that
"Melchizedek had a good innate knowledge of the true God."

Wilhelm Albrecht Teller (1734-1804), in his oft-reprinted
NT wordbook,[1] sought confirmation of his naturalistic for-
mulation of religion via appeal to the words and idiomatic
expressions of Scripture. Teller argues that the pure kernel
of religion may be extracted from Scripture by translating
the ancient Oriental religious ideas preserved in the words
of the NT into modern Occidental thought forms.

The significance of Melchizedek is bound up in the title
"priest of the Most High God" (vs. 1), which in the OT occurs only in Gen 14:18. Teller argues that reason plus Oriental philosophy yield ideas which give substance to the un-
garnished words of the text. Thus if the interpreter is able
to deduce from Oriental wisdom the fundamental idea behind
the title "priest of the Most High God," he will gain understanding of Melchizedek and his role as a religious leader.
The priest historically exercised the function of a servant

---

1) *Wörterbuch des Neuen Testaments zur Erklärung des christlichen
Lehre* (Berlin, 1792[5]), 345 ff.

or counsellor in the court of the monarch. For the sake of
the Jews who were accustomed to the Levitical ritual cultus,
the apostle accommodated his conception of the Oriental civil servant to the more familiar thought forms of the Mosaic
system. Teller returns to Eastern philosophy for guidance
as to the unique contribution made by this servant of the
Highest. Porphyry of Tyre (III AD) suggests that the servant
of the Most High possessed esoteric knowledge of the means,
whereby man gains access to God. Likewise the Neoplatonist
philosopher Iamblichus (III/IV AD) describes the servant of
the Most High as "a rational worshipper of God" who communes
with deity without recourse to an elaborate ritual apparatus.
Similarly Philo depicted Melchizedek as one who "had sublime
and dignified conceptions of God." Together these authorities illustrate the central feature of Melchizedek's religious genius: the Salemite priest, as servant of the Most
High God, was the forebearer of a perfectly moral and rational religion. Melchizedek himself was the model rationalist!

> He had noble conceptions of the true God, not only that
> God exists but also that he would be the God of Abraham,
> even though he (Melchizedek) belonged to another people,
> and that he would disseminate his blessings upon all
> peoples.

The commentary of Johann Heinrich Heinrichs,[1] published
in 1792 while the author was a tutor at Göttingen, also characterizes our text as an allegorical argument accommodated
to the fantasies of the ancient Jews. Proceeding from the
Jewish belief based on Psa 110:4 that Melchizedek foreshadowed
the eternal priesthood of the Messiah, Hebrews freely im-
mortalizes the type as one whose origin was unknown and who
would be a priest for all times (vs. 3). The clause ὅτι ζῇ
(vs. 8) is yet a further concession to the Jewish superstition that Melchizedek would exercise a perpetual priesthood
in the heavenly realm. Heinrich's estimate of Hebrews' *ad
hominem* argument is tersely put: "What an extraordinary sense
of imagination! What unbridled extravagance!"

---

1) *Pauli epistola ad Hebraeos graece, perpetua adnotatione illustrata*,
vol. VIII of J.B. Koppe's *Novum Testamentum graece* (Göttingen, 1823[2]),
110 ff.

4. *THE NINETEENTH CENTURY*

(a) Rationalistic Interpretation (cont'd)

Nineteenth century rationalism, like that of the previous
century, was a multiheaded hydra which manifested itself in
a variety of forms. Seemingly more governed by the thought
of contemporary thinkers such as Kant (d. 1804) and Hegel
(d. 1831) than by Christian theology in its historical development, the work of a rationalist interpreter of the period reads more like a text of speculative philosophical theology than a traditional biblical commentary. The rationalists often presupposed the thoroughgoing accommodation of
antiquated Jewish traditions and Oriental superstitions in
order to argue Jesus' eminence as bearer of a higher moral
religion. Typical is the argument of Kuinoel (1768-1841),
that the process whereby a simple OT narrative (Gen 14:17 ff.)
is allegorized into a far more sublime argument (Heb 7:1 ff.)
"smells entirely like rabbinic hermeneutics."[1] Whereas earlier rationalism emptied much of the content of the Christian faith, one strand of later rationalism proceeded a stage
further to the logical conclusion of denying the very existence of Christianity as an historical institution. A faith
whose cardinal tenets had been discarded soon led to a faith
the existence of which was forthwith denied.

The Breslau theologian David Schulz (1779-1854) was for
many years a bulwark of theological rationalism in Germany.
His principal contribution to biblical exegesis was a translation of Hebrews with appended introduction and commentary.[2]
Schulz advances the thesis that Hebrews has no conception of
a Levitical cultus which had been abrogated by the priesthood of Christ. Discounting the likelihood of the independent
existence of Christianity on earth, Schulz argues that its
reality consists in the promise of a greater glory which
would be realized in the age to come when the old earthly
cultus would give way to the heavenly priesthood of the Mes-

---

1) *Commentarius in Epistolam ad Hebraeos* (Leipzig, 1831), 223.
2) *Der Brief an die Hebräer; Einleitung, Übersetzung und Anmerkungen*
(Breslau, 1818), 74 ff.

siah presently held in store. The latter represents the ren-
ovation and consummation of the former, embodying its highest
ideals. Early in the history of the Old Covenant the Jews
saw in the priest-king of Salem one who prefigured the en-
during priesthood of the Messiah in the new age.

By depicting Melchizedek as ἀπάτωρ, κτλ the author wished
to express that the ancient type of the Messiah "ought to
be regarded as one who originated from God himself and not
from any earthly parents." As the offspring of God's direct
creative activity, Melchizedek came into existence independently of human parentage in contrast to the legal priests
who were required to prove descent from Levi. Furthermore,
μένει ἱερεὺς κτλ is to be understood not in a figurative
sense, but in the strictly literal sense that Melchizedek
actually lives on as a priest for ever. By exercising a perpetual priestly ministration, Melchizedek most suitably adumbrates the heavenly priesthood of the Messiah. The fact
that the author portrays Melchizedek as a supramundane figure begotten independently of normal human procreation does
not guarantee commitment to that view either by the writer
of Hebrews or by our interpreter. On the contrary, Hebrews
contrived the farfetched argument by way of concession to
the current expectation of the ancient Jews who regarded
Melchizedek as a type of the future heavenly Messiah. Accordingly, μαρτυρούμενος ὅτι ζῆ signifies that amongst the
Jews Melchizedek "had the good testimony or commendation"
that he was endowed with such an imperishable life.

Christian Friedrich Böhme,[1] pastor at Altenburg, was
trained in the school of older rationalism. Böhme likewise
argued that the author of Hebrews subtly allegorized the OT
Melchizedek pericope to accommodate his argument to the superstitions of first century Jews. Hence with one eye on his
readers, the writer of Hebrews came to the extraordinary
conclusion that, like the Son of God, Melchizedek also came
into the world without human ancestry (ἀπάτωρ, κτλ), that
his life which knew no bounds (μήτε ἀρχὴν ἡμερῶν κτλ) was

---

1) *Epistola ad Hebraeos latine vertit atque commentario instruxit
perpetuo* (Leipzig, 1825), 290 ff.

eternal, and that consequently he exercises his priesthood
for ever (μένει ἱερεὺς κτλ). Hebrews' exegesis, therefore,
perfectly agrees with that of the Psalmist who likened the
eternal Messiah to the Salemite monarch. The affirmation
that Melchizedek ζῆ (vs. 8) could be regarded as synonymous
with the declaration μένει ἱερεὺς κτλ. On the other hand,
the positive affirmation ζῆ could also have been deduced from
the more restrained negative statement μήτε ζωῆς τέλος ἔχων,
in which case Hebrews' exegesis would "smell of the odor of
the rabbis." Thus because Melchizedek, who in his eternity
remarkably adumbrates Christ, is vastly superior to the Levitical priests, so is the Christian religion more noble
than Judaism.

Popularly acclaimed "the true patriarch of rationalism,"[1]
the Heidelberg theologian Heinrich E. G. Paulus (1761-1851)
represents the pinnacle of nineteenth century German theological rationalism. Paulus' marked rationalism took shape
during his early years. Reacting against the spiritualist
practices of his father, a minister in the Evangelical Church,
Heinrich became distrustful of all religious phenomena anti-
thetic to reason. His later associations with the rationalistic philosophers Herder (d. 1803) and Hegel (d. 1831) further crystallized his theological convictions. Characterized
by one colleague as "a man who thinks that he believes and
believes that he thinks,"[2] Paulus wrote a commentary on Hebrews[3] which evinces all the features of classical rationalism.

Paul's intimate knowledge of the turn of mind of his Jew-
ish-Christian brethren assured him that as soon as mention
was made of the name of the mysterious Gentile priest-king,
their minds would be drawn with rapt attention to the striking similarity between Melchizedek and Jesus. The apostle's
allegorical explication of Melchizedek's proper name and
title (vs. 2) highlights a striking likeness between the

---

1) F. Lichtenburger, *History of German Theology in the Nineteenth
Century* (Edinburgh, 1889), 21.

2) *ADB*, XXV, 293.

3) *Des Apostels Paulus Ermahnungs-Schreiben an die Hebräer-Christen*
(Heidelberg, 1833), 76 ff.

two figures. Βασιλεὺς δικαιοσύνης suggests not the imputa-
tion of divine righteousness, but the moral perfection of
Jesus' kingdom. Similarly, βασιλεὺς εἰρήνης signifies the
all-embracing "peace with God, with one's self and with all
good men and spirits" which proceeds from the religion of
Jesus.

A further likeness is forged by the *ad hominem* allegory
of vs. 3, which was devised to underscore Jesus' affinity
with the Messiah of Jewish expectation. Paulus argues:

> Undoubtedly the author in his own mind referred these
> particulars to the "Messiasgeist" embodied in Jesus, in
> respect of which neither origin, nor beginning, nor
> end of life could be given up, which earmarks him as
> God's Messiah and son.

The term "Messiasgeist" is repeatedly employed as a designation of the Messianic character of the Melchizedekian shadow.
Contemporary philosophical idealism influenced Paulus' conception of Jesus as a mere man in whom the *Geist* of the Messiah found its abode.[1] Paulus sought to substantiate this
theological presupposition from demonstrable historical data.
Thus he argued that during the period of the Maccabees the
idea of an earthly Messianic kingdom administered by a Da-
vidic descendant weakened. Instead there arose the idea of
the Messiah as a heavenly guardian spirit whose rule was administered from the celestial realm. The writer of Hebrews
transferred this strand of Messianic expectation upon Jesus
so as to extol him as the underregent of a new moral and
rational religion.[2] Hence "Messiasgeist" relates to the heavenly, Messianic spirit divinely implanted in the human Jesus,
from which his royal and priestly authority are derived.[3]
The notion of the spirit of the Messiah embodied in the human Jesus was not inimical to Paulus' naturalistic concep-

---

1) Paulus' conception of the Messianic spirit was likely influenced
by Hegel's idea of "Geist." In terms of the incarnation, Hegel constructed the following dialectic: *thesis*, God as divine unity; *antithesis*,
finite human nature; *higher synthesis*, Jesus the God-man. See W. Walker,
A History of the Christian Church (New York, 1959), 489.

2) See Paulus, *Das Leben Jesu als Grundlage einer reinen Geschichte
des Urchristentums* (2 vols.; Heidelberg, 1828), I, 47 ff.

3) See L.F.O. Baumgarten-Crusius, *Grundzüge der biblischen Theologie*
(Jena, 1828), 382 ff. for further discussion of the heavenly origin of
the "Messiasgeist" in Jesus.

tion of a non-unique Jesus or of the Christian religion:
"that such a spirit should be found in a human body is itself a miracle."[1]

(b) Critical Commentaries

The growing conviction early in the nineteenth century
that rationalistic interpretation with its manifold subjective preconceptions had led biblical science into a blind
alley, prompted scholars to return to the more secure moor-
ings of a philological, grammatical and historical interpretation of the NT. Although critical interpreters approached
Hebrews with diverse theological presuppositions, their fundamental concern was to uncover the design of the author and
the meaning of the text in relation to those to whom it was
directed. Thus critical commentators of the period often
posed the question: "Was will der Verfasser hiermit sagen?"
In quest of an unbiased explication of the text, commentators engaged in exacting philological analyses of difficult
words and phrases, citing parallels from both extra-biblical
and biblical sources. Careful attention was also given to
the religious, cultural and historical milieu of the writing.
Theological considerations, although not of paramount concern, were not entirely overlooked, hence the occasional
doctrinal excursus interspersed amidst the exegesis. In short,
the rejection of the subjectivity and frivolity of the former age in favor of the more certain ground of objective
scientific exegesis yielded some of the most illuminating
commentaries on Hebrews ever prepared.

Popularly acclaimed the father of American biblical literature, Moses Stuart (1780-1852) held the chair of Sacred
Literature at the Andover Seminary, Massachusetts, for nearly
four decades. Committed to the scientific study of Scripture
within the framework of orthodox theology, Stuart was one
of the first American interpreters to be thoroughly acquainted with critical European biblical scholarship. Stuart's
highly regarded Hebrews commentary,[2] which passed through

---

1) *Leben Jesu*, I, xi.
2) *A Commentary on the Epistle to the Hebrews* (London, 1837), 365 ff.

four editions, was undertaken to counter the growing influence of European neology in orthodox theological circles in the English speaking world.[1]

Heb 7:1 ff. is regarded as an *argumentum ad hominem* advanced to counter belief in the ultimate validity of the Mosaic religion. Thus Stuart suggests that the argument based on genealogy and descent is of little relevance to the modern reader, since "we have now more convincing arguments than those here used, to establish the superiority of Christ's priesthood." The author's main purpose in allegorizing the OT history of Melchizedek was to demonstrate that the new order of priesthood was not confined to any fixed period of time. Hence μήτε ἀρχὴν ἡμερῶν κτλ affirms that unlike the Levites, the commencement and termination of whose service was prescribed in the law, Melchizedek "had no limited time assigned for the commencement and expiration of his office." That the writer has in view the continuance of the priesthood and not the person himself, is clear from the precise parallelism drawn in vs. 8. Applied to the Levites, ἀποθνῄσκοντες ἄνθρωποι could hardly refer to the demise of their persons, since they were no less mortal than the king of Salem. Both, in fact, could be said to be immortal in terms of their continuance in the world to come. But if we correctly comprehend the phrase in terms of "the brief and mutable condition of the Levitical priesthood," then "the undelimited continuance of the priesthood of Melchizedek and hence of Christ is thereby demonstrated."

One of the most distinguished interpreters of Hebrews of all times, Friedrich Bleek (1793-1859) was for three decades professor of theology at Bonn, where he supported orthodox interpretation during the ascendency of the radical Tübingen school of F. C. Baur. His eminence as a biblical critic and

---

1) In the publisher's preface to the 1828 English edition, E. Henderson remarks: "The ordeal to which it (ie, Hebrews) has been subjected by the wild and extravagant hypotheses of some of the master spirits of Germany rendered it a matter of imperious necessity that it should be submitted to a fresh and full investigation." Similarly, the preface to the 1837 English edition refers to the "turbid streams of neologism and Socinianism, and . . . the strong bias of the master spirits of German sacred literature" to which English readers have been exposed.

exegete was due to his expansive learning, sound judgment
and acute historical consciousness. Bleek's exhaustive three-
volume commentary on Hebrews[1] advocates a boldly literal approach to our text.

Melchizedek was an authentic personality from the primitive history who prefigured the person and office of the NT
high priest. Vs. 3, which unlocks the meaning of the passage
as a whole, scarcely permits the figurative *argumentum e
silentio* often advanced. Ἀγενεαλόγητος implies that Melchizedek's entry into the world was other than via the usual
process of human generation. Μήτε ἀρχὴν ἡμερῶν κτλ, particularly when viewed in context with ἀπάτωρ, ἀμήτωρ, denotes
the literal absence of beginning and end of natural life.
These negative declarations suggest that Melchizedek did not
succumb to death, much as Enoch and Elijah who were translated to heaven.

> These predicates must be understood in a manner other
> than the usual assumption. They refer not merely to the
> silence of the history concerning the birth and descent
> of Melchizedek . . . , but they suggest that he really
> had no human parents and ancestors at all. Thus we pro-
> pose that he was placed upon earth and later removed
> directly by divine omnipotence, as an incarnation of
> a divine spirit or, at least, of a heavenly being.

Granted that μένει ἱερεὺς κτλ refers to the uninterrupted
priesthood of the miraculously conceived heavenly being,
Bleek seeks to determine the precise *terminus ad quem* of his
priestly service. The supposition that Melchizedek exercises
his ministration indefinitely would bring his priesthood into collision with that of Christ. Bleek advances the conjecture that "the priestly activity of the type extended to
that point in time where the priestly ministry of the antitype entered, that is, up to the heavenly exaltation of the
Son of God." That Melchizedek continued to exercise priestly
functions even *after* his translation via divine power from
earth to heaven is supported by ὅτι ζῇ (vs. 8). In contrast
with the Levitical priests who die and thus succeed one another, witness is borne of Melchizedek by an extant Jewish
tradition that he was endowed with a life which continues on

---

1) *Der Brief an die Hebräer* (3 vols.; Berlin, 1828-40), III, 281 ff.

untouched by death.

Heinrich G. A. Ewald (1803-75) was one of the foremost biblical scholars of the nineteenth century. Avoiding allegiance with the rationalists and with traditional confessional theologians, Ewald struck an independent path in biblical research. In opposition to the school of F. C. Baur (but not without neological emphases of his own), Ewald wrote commentaries on most of the NT including the Epistle to the Hebrews.[1] Not unexpectedly, the biblical interpretation of the independently minded orientalist reflects mystical and cosmological elements borrowed from the extra-biblical literature of the East. That Ewald's exegesis includes arbitrary and fanciful results may be attributed to his judgment that the author closely followed Philo, who regarded Melchizedek as a manifestation of the divine Logos.

Heb 7:1 ff. is founded upon the mysterious sounding Psalm text, which itself is a concise commentary on the odd and enigmatic Genesis 14 narrative. A plain reading of our text leads to the conclusion that the writer thought of the Salemite not as an ordinary human, but as a transcendent immortal figure. Thus ἀπάτωρ, κτλ is to be interpreted in the *prima facie* literal sense that Melchizedek was devoid of human parentage, and that any attempt to retrace his family lineage would be a forelorn hope. Similarly, μήτε ἀρχὴν ἡμερῶν κτλ asserts that Melchizedek's life had neither a beginning nor an end in time, as with ordinary mortals. Ewald thus concludes that

> Melchizedek would be Christ, or rather the Logos who in the primitive history manifested himself to men in that particular form. Furthermore, he was at the time of his early manifestation a priest by way of intimation of that which he now is in a wholly different way--an eternal high priest for his own.

Melchizedek's identity as "a momentary, mysterious and bodily manifestation of the Logos who had dropped down, as it were, into that early antiquity" is confirmed by the witness of both the Genesis and Psalm texts: ὅτι ζῇ (vs. 8) implies that Melchizedek "lives on" perpetually in precisely the

---

1) *Das Sendschreiben an die Hebräer und Jakobos' Rundschreiben übersetzt und erklärt* (Göttingen, 1870), 86 ff.

same sense that "Christ himself as the Logos is called the
'living' one according to Heb 4:12."[1]

In his popular edition of the Greek NT[2] Henry Alford (1810-
71), former Dean of Canterbury, likewise favors the strictly
literal interpretation of our text. Melchizedek, who was
providentially set forth as a mysterious type of Christ, was
a figure fundamentally different from the ordinary course of
humanity. Thus μήτε ἀρχὴν ἡμερῶν κτλ is most naturally understood in the sense that Melchizedek's existence had neither a beginning nor end. Discounting the interpretation
based on the silence of the OT, Alford comments: "It really
would seem to me almost childish to say thus solemnly of any
whose acts were related in the OT, but whose birth and death
were not related, that 'they had neither beginning of days
nor end of life.'"

Unlike Bleek, Ewald and others who saw in Melchizedek a
heavenly angel being or Christ himself, Alford judges that
the portrait of Melchizedek in Heb 7:1 ff. conceals an un-
fathomable mystery which shall be revealed only in the here-
after. Hence the enigma of Melchizedek is a matter about
which the interpreter ought not trouble himself: "It is one
of those things in which we must not be wise above that which
is written, but must take simply and trustingly the plain
sense of our Bibles on a deep and mysterious subject and
leave it for the day when all shall be clear."

In contrast with the preceding interpreters who gave a
literal interpretation of Heb 7:1 ff., a thoroughgoing symbolic explication was advanced by Wilhelm M. L. de Wette
(1780-1849), one of the outstanding exegetes of the century.
His theological outlook was shaped by his Jena teacher H.
E. G. Paulus and by his association with Schleiermacher at
Berlin. De Wette adopted a mediating position in relation

---

1) "For the word of God is living and active, sharper than any two-
edged sword. . . ." Ewald characteristically tended to idealize eminent
OT personalities. As O. Pfleiderer observed: "When any historical figure
impresses him . . . , he is immediately carried away by his feelings,
and ascribes to his heroes, forgetting the requirements of sober criticism, all the noble moral thoughts and feelings which he, the historian,
entertains at the moment." *The Development of Theology* (London, 1893[2]),
257.

2) *The Greek Testament* (4 vols.; London, 1863-66[2]), IV, 125 ff.

to rationalism and supernaturalism; his denunciation of un-
aided reason offended the older rationalists, whereas his
extensive critical pursuits incurred the opposition of the
pietists. De Wette had little patience with a religion founded on reason or, for that matter, on historical evidences
alone: Instead he sought to transcend the strictly objective
data of religion and apprehend the supernatural through the
medium of subjective feeling by faith. Far too transcendent
to be grasped by finite modes of expression, the supernatural or aesthetic side of religion is amenable only to symbolic representation. Where de Wette was compelled to reject
certain supernatural aspects of Scripture, he interpreted
the phenomena as mythical elements which nevertheless convey sublime truths. His theological works include a valuable
essay on the symbolico-typical teaching of Hebrews[1] and a
concise exegetical commentary on the NT.[2]

De Wette opposed the rationalists' view that Heb 7:1 ff.
is an *argumentum e concessu* and hence lacks objective validity.[3] Rather the New Covenant, as the larger of two concen-
tric circles, represents the fulfillment and consummation of
the Old. Thus such OT entities such as high priest, sacrifice, etc. are embryonic symbols of New Covenant realities.
De Wette emphasized the need to gain a correct understanding
of the typological significance of Melchizedek before attempting an exegesis of our text. He argued that Melchizedek
would be a "Vorbild" of a different sort than the aforemen-
tioned OT symbols (high priest, etc.) since he lies outside
the sphere of the Mosaic economy. The most that can be affirmed is that "Melchizedek was a mythico-historical figure
of the general religious history of the OT."[4] The Salemite

---

1) "Über die symbolisch-typische Lehrart des Briefes an die Hebräer,"
Theologische Zeitschrift, hrsg. Schleiermacher, de Wette & Lücke (3
vols.; Berlin, 1818-22), III, 1-57.
2) *Kurzgefasstes exegetisches Handbuch zum Neuen Testament* (3 vols.;
Leipzig, 1838-48[2]). Heb 7:1 ff. in II, v, 186 ff.
3) *Theologische Zeitschrift*, III, 2 ff. De Wette admits that he once
held to the accommodation theory, but thereafter came to realize that
"the teaching method of the writer of Hebrews is, to be sure, allegorical and symbolical, but on no account is it arbitrary and worthless.
It still holds for me genuine living meaning."
4) *Ibid.*, III, 25.

priest-king, the account of whom is derived from an uncertain ancient legend, enters the sphere of OT symbolism solely on the basis of the Psalmist's declaration that he would be a type of the theocratic king.

Hebrews' portrait of Melchizedek, sketched to provide a biblical foundation for the NT high priest, appears incompatible with that of a historical personage. But de Wette maintains that the writer of Hebrews was unconscious of any disparity between the historical and the symbolical Melchizedek; his attention focused solely upon the one who according to Psa 110:4 symbolically depicts the eternal priest of the New Covenant. De Wette's explication of this symbolic Melchizedek is all too brief. Ἀπάτωρ, κτλ affirms that nothing is known from the OT record of his immediate family, forefathers or descendants. His priesthood is founded not on lineage or priestly succession, but solely on his own personal worth. Vs. 3 in no wise delineates detailed ontological statements about the person of Christ; such a practice introduces theological problems which in any case are irrelevant to the purpose at hand. The absence of beginning and end of life establishes the Salemite as a model of the eternity of Christ's person and priesthood. The troublesome clause μένει ἱερεὺς κτλ gives up its meaning only when viewed in the light of the Melchizedek-Christ typology. De Wette cautions against restricting the clause to something less than a proper eternity. Neither do the words signify the eternity of Melchizedek, otherwise the priesthood of the latter would impinge upon that of Christ. De Wette regards the foregoing as a purely *typological* notion of ultimate reference to Christ alone. Absence of beginning and end of Melchizedek's priestly ministration was utilized to portray symbolically the absolute eternity of the priesthood of Christ. Hence affirmations made in respect of Melchizedek realize their intended meaning when viewed in terms of Christ.

A thoroughgoing symbolic interpretation of our text was likewise advocated by the Halle mediating theologian F. A. G. Tholuck (1799-1877).[1] Noting that Christ and the apostles

---

1) *Kommentar zum Briefe an die Hebräer* (Hamburg, 1850[3]), 287 ff.

frequently conveyed profound spiritual truth in the form of
symbolism, Tholuck argues that Heb 7:1 ff. expounds not the
historical Melchizedek but the symbolic or typical figure
whose main features were stimulated by the prophetic declaration of Psa 110:4. The shroud of mystery which surrounds
his origin in Genesis 14 endows Melchizedek with the timelessness of a supra-human being. Nevertheless the symbolic
statements of Heb 7:1 ff., affirming Melchizedek's unique
origin and eternity *a parte ante* and *a parte post*, are absolutely valid only in relation to Christ the higher reality
whom he symbolizes. Argues Tholuck: "Who can believe that
a Christian apostle would attribute to Melchizedek an eternal existence in the same way as he would ascribe it to God's
only begotten Son?" Thus Hebrews' bold declarations about
Melchizedek's eternal existence and perpetuity in priesthood (vss. 3, 8), are understandable only in the sense of
the eternal continuance of the type in the antitype. Expressed
otherwise, the affirmations made in respect of Melchizedek
are true in the sense that they are absolutely true of Christ.

Eduard Wilhelm Reuss (1804-91), who taught theology for
more than half a century at Strasbourg, in addition to major historical works prepared a French translation with commentary of Old and New Testaments.[1] Fundamentally a historian rather than a dogmatician, Reuss held that painstaking
historical research was a necessary requisite to biblical
exegesis. Reuss' historical studies led to a radical depreciation of the historical reality of the Gen 14:17 ff. account and to a concomitant emphasis upon the extensive theological implications of the primitive narrative.

Hebrews' subtle spiritualizing of the obscure Genesis
pericope endowed Melchizedek with a typical and ideal existence. The proper name of the person (Μελχισέδεκ) and place
(Σαλήμ) were set forth not as fortuitous personal and geographical designations, but as fundamental *theological concepts*. Thus "righteousness" and "peace" are two principal
characteristics of the Christian gospel.

---

1) "L'Épître aux Hébreux," in *La Bible: Nouveau Testament* (6 vols.;
Paris, 1876-78), V, 59 ff.

The author is not the least bit concerned, like many exegetes, to determine the location of the city of Salem. He knows that the city of peace exists only in heaven. The king of this city can only be the Son of God.

Furthermore, ἀπάτωρ, κτλ portrays Melchizedek as one wholly detached from the sphere of human history. That is, the Alexandrian author's allegorico-typical interpretation was not intended "to relate a more or less curious scene in the life of a man," but to draw attention to the eternal attributes of the Son of God. Indeed, ἀφωμοιωμένος κτλ identifies Melchizedek as a "type" or "image" of God's Son, and not as an independent figure in the primitive history.

> Melchizedek is not a historic personality, but a typical figure. For what is said in vs. 3 is not true of any man, not even the man Jesus, who at least had a mother and a genealogy, who was born on one day and died on another. But that is true of the Son of God, for whom the notions of fatherhood, birth, etc., do not have the usual meaning, whose existence exceeds the bounds of time at both ends.

With Melchizedek elevated above the temporal and historical and posited in the realm of the theological, Reuss concludes that "the record in Genesis was not a narrative, but a doctrinal statement."[1]

The conservative OT scholar Franz Delitzsch (1813-90)[2] commends the traditional view that via an *argumentum e silentio* Melchizedek is set forth as an historical type of Christ's person and priesthood. Since Delitzsch follows rather closely the exegesis of his fellow Lutheran J. C. von Hofmann,[3] it is sufficient to point out that Melchizedek is identified as a threefold prefiguration of Christ. The first is the union of priesthood and royalty in a figure characterized by righteousness and peace. Even the seemingly triv-

---

1) *Histoire de la Théologie chrétienne au Siècle apostolique* (2 vols.; Strasbourg & Paris, 1864[3]), II, 276. Reuss argues that Hebrews could never have regarded Melchizedek as an historical person: "From the moment that Melchizedek would be anything else (ie, than a symbol of Christ) the entire argument of the author would crumble, for then there would have been, apart from Christ, a man who could have received the honors solely reserved for the Son of God." "L'Épître aux Hébreux," 61.

2) *Commentar zum Briefe an die Hebräer* (Leipzig, 1857), 265 ff.

3) See below, pp. 84 ff. Delitzsch, however, frequently takes issue with von Hofmann's view of the person of Christ and the atonement.

ial details of Melchizedek's name and seat of his rule were ordained by Providence as pregnant symbols of the coming Messiah. Second, ἀπάτωρ, ἀμήτωρ suggests that Melchizedek was endowed with an official dignity founded upon inherent worth rather than upon circumstances of fleshly descent. The opinion of older orthodox interpreters that the pair of epithets depict the fatherless humanity and the motherless divinity of our Lord must be set aside as lacking foundation. Finally, absence of data concerning Melchizedek's birth and decease symbolically portrays the absolute eternity of Christ, from which it follows that his priesthood transcends time. In response to von Hofmann, Delitzsch insists that Hebrews chose the title υἱὸς τοῦ θεοῦ (vs. 3) rather than χριστός, for example, to emphasize that the incarnate priest of the New Covenant, "by virtue of his community of essence with the Father" has neither beginning nor end of personal existence.

According to Johann Heinrich Kurtz (1809-90),[1] professor of OT and church history at Dorpat, the typical and idealized portrait of Melchizedek stimulated by the Messianic Psalm text symbolizes the high priestly dignity of the eternal Son of God. The negative statements, ἀπάτωρ, ἀμήτωρ, ἀγενεαλόγητος, which apply to Melchizedek only in a derivative sense, highlight the mystery of the eternal existence and divinity of Christ, who is devoid of father, mother, beginning and end.

A kind of *character indelebilis* is ascribed to the type by μένει ἱερεὺς κτλ, which is to be understood in the idealized sense of the continuance of the priestly character without the exercise of priestly functions. Thus Kurtz argues: "the sacerdotal activity of a priest comes to an end, whereas his priestly character yet remains." Although Melchizedek died, nevertheless, having no successors in office his priesthood clings to his person and thus "continues on" (ζῇ, vs. 8).

Brooke Foss Westcott (1825-1901) ranks as one of the foremost English biblical exegetes of modern times. The Hebrews

---

1) *Der Brief an die Hebräer erklärt* (Mitau, 1869), 218 ff.

commentary[1] of the Regius Professor of Divinity at Cambridge
is widely recognized as a model of philological, grammatical
and historical exegesis. Westcott's deep esteem for the interpretive results of the fathers and later Christian scholars has endowed his commentaries with a certain catholicity
which avoids novel conclusions. The single point at which
his exegesis may be faulted is his tendency to overexpound
the text, occasionally inserting nuances of meaning which
the text itself hardly sustains.[2]

Westcott surmises that Melchizedek was likely an Amorite
priest-king who was the unique bearer of a primitive revelation. Yet the intent of Hebrews was not to unfold the life
and personality of the historical figure (as if to enquire,
"Who and what was Melchizedek?"), but to expound the biblical portrait of the primitive priest. Noting that the silence of the Genesis narrative, as well as its positive declarations, embodies great prophetic power, Westcott identifies Melchizedek as a threefold type of Christ: (i) in
character, as "king of righteousness and king of peace" (vs.
2); (ii) in *office*, as bearer of a unique, non-Levitical
priesthood; and (iii) in *person* or *nature*, in terms of the
absence of recorded birth and death. Westcott's inclination
to elicit subtle distinctions which exceed the warrant of
the text is illustrated by his explication of the phrase
μήτε ἀρχὴν ἡμερῶν κτλ. The wording as it stands in the text,
rather than the more direct expression μήτε ἀρχὴν μήτε τέλος
ζωῆς suggests wider Christological implications.

> Perhaps the remarkable variation in the language, which
> cannot be mere rhetorical ornament . . . , may point to
> the fact that the Son of God was (in His *Divine Nature*)
> beyond time, while the *human life* which He assumed was
> to be without end.

Hermann von Soden (1852-1914), the German textual critic
and interpreter of Scripture, was professor of divinity at
the University of Berlin. He contributed commentaries to
Holtzmann's *Hand-Commentar zum Neuen Testament* on selected

---

1) *The Epistle to the Hebrews* (London, 1892[2]), 170 ff.
2) C.J. Vaughan expresses this tendency of Westcott most succinctly:
"When he reaps his field, he leaves no corners of it for the gleaner."
Epistle to the Hebrews (London, 1890), vi.

Pauline Epistles, the General Epistles as well as Hebrews.[1]

By the turn of the century one of the 'assured' results
of NT criticism was acceptance of the thoroughgoing dependence of Hebrews upon Philo. Von Soden likewise maintained
that Hebrews is dominated by linguistic and conceptual motifs from first century Alexandrian theology. Neither a
Paulinist nor a representative of Palestinian Judaism, the
author of Hebrews was "a skillfully trained representative
of the school of Alexandrian Judaism as it was classically
embodied in the person of Philo." After his conversion to
Christianity the Alexandrian writer used Philonic concepts
to more fully interpret the gospel of Christ. According to
von Sodon, "It is quite certain that one cannot understand
Hebrews without Philo." Thus in the course of his reflection on the high priesthood of Christ, the writer of Hebrews (motivated by the Philonic Logos teaching[2]) gave a
fresh reinterpretation of the relevant Genesis and Psalm
texts and applied them to Christ via an allegorical exegesis befitting a Christian Philonist.

The issue of paramount importance for von Soden is the
manner in which Hebrews transferred to Christ relevant features of Alexandrian theology and how he filled these concepts with Christian content. Melchizedek resembles the Son
of God in two respects: (i) according to his "Wirken," on
the basis of Philo's designation of the Salemite as "the
righteous king" and "king of peace";[3] (ii) according to his
"Wesen," lacking beginning and end of life. In the latter
case, since Philo regarded Melchizedek as a manifestation
of the θεῖος λόγος,[4] and since he further described the latter as a υἱὸς θεοῦ,[5] von Soden judges that Hebrews likens
Melchizedek not to the historical Jesus, but to the heavenly

---

1) "Der Brief an die Hebräer," *HCNT* III.2 (Freiburg i.B., 1899[3]), 56 ff
2) "The Philonic 'Logologie' is the armoury for the Christology of
Hebrews." However, the rigid dualism between the infinite and finite
worlds of Philo has been spanned by the high priest after the order of
Melchizedek who became flesh in order to qualify for mediatorial service. In the person of the incarnate Son of God, "theosophy is changed
into religion."
3) *Leg. alleg.* III. 79.
4) *De somn.* I. 215.
5) *De confus. ling.* 146; cf. *De agric.* 51.

Lord--ie, to the Son of God in his "vor - und nachirdischen
Existenz." Thus the predicates of vs. 3 concerning Jesus'
origin and descent refer not to his entry into earthly life,
but pre-eminently delineate the supra-temporal (ie, preincarnate and glorified) existence of the Logos or Son of God.

Thomas Kelly Cheyne (1841-1915),[1] who studied at Göttingen
under H. G. A. Ewald and who later became Oriel Professor
of the Interpretation of Scripture at Oxford, advanced radically unconventional theories of biblical criticism. Cheyne
argues that the OT Melchizedek pericope, Gen 14:18-20, represents the post-exilic editorial interpolation of an un-
reliable and unhistorical narrative. As it stands, Gen 14:
18 ff. reflects a later scribe's best attempt to make sense
out of a poorly copied insertion to the text. The other supposed Melchizedek citation, Psa 110:4, is no less corrupt.
Instead of the received reading, "You are a priest for ever
after the order of Melchizedek," the original text probably
read, "I have established thee for ever because of my loving
kindness." The name of Melchizedek was carelessly appended
to the Psalm citation by a later hand. Thus Cheyne judges
that "Melchizedek . . . is a purely fictitious personage,
introduced for some object which is yet to be discovered."

As for the development of the theme in Heb 7:1 ff., Cheyne
argues that "the author of the Epistle to the Hebrews . . .
treats the short account of Melchizedek in Genesis 14 as a
mine of suggestion for the right comprehension of the nature
and office of Christ." The piece of post-exilic redaction
(Gen 14:18-20) became the basis for the elaborate typolo-
gizing which, because of its obsession with the letter of
a spurious OT text, must be regarded as "mere temporary
rhetoric."

(c) Biblical Theologians

The determination of critical exegetes to avoid the domination of biblical interpretation by preconceived dogma
prompted investigations which were primarily philological,

---

1) "Melchizedek," *Encyclopaedia Biblica* (4 vols.; London: 1899-1903),
III, 3014 ff.

grammatical and historical in character. The results of such
an exegetical approach, however, were frequently lean in
theological content. Critical enquiry had gone far towards
answering the question, "What did the text mean in relation
to those to whom it was directed?" but detailed consideration of the theology of the text remained outside the scope
of the average critical commentary. The so-called 'biblical
theologians' sought to redress this imbalance by constructing
a total biblical theology of the Epistle. This is not to
suggest that the exegetical method of scholarly nineteenth
century biblical theologians was lacking in critical acumen;
frequently their exegesis manifests many of the features
common to scientific biblical scholarship of the period.
Their distinctiveness resides in the fact that via a topi-
cal arrangement of the relevant texts they strove to bring
together under a single subject heading the various strands
of a given theme.

One of the most influential nineteenth century biblical
theologians was the Erlangen scholar Johann Christian von
Hofmann (1810-77). In addition to a commentary on Hebrews[1]
he wrote a capital work on biblical theology[2] which became
highly controversial because of its departure from the traditional Lutheran doctrine of the person and atoning work
of Christ. Hofmann's principal concern in our text is to
counter the orthodox practice of deducing from the Melchizedek interpretation ontological statements about Christ. The
title υἱὸς τοῦ θεοῦ (vs. 3) witnesses not to the divine and
eternal Son, but to Jesus' human and temporal relation to
the Father. From this theological presupposition he argues
that vs. 3 depicts Melchizedek and Christ in their *priestly*
rather than in their personal capacities. Thus whereas most
interpreters view μήτε ἀρχὴν ἡμερῶν κτλ in terms of the personal life of Melchizedek, and deduce therefrom the eternity
of Christ, Hofmann sees in the foregoing expression only the

---

1) "Der Brief an die Hebräer," *Die Heilige Schrift neuen Testaments
zusammenhängend untersucht* (9 vols.; Nordlingen, 1862-78), V, 260 ff.
2) *Der Schriftbeweis: ein theologischer Versuch* (2 vols.; Nordlingen,
1857-60[2]).

absence of recorded entry into priesthood and termination
of sacerdotal life. Had the writer wished to characterize
the *persons* of the two priestly figures, he probably would
have employed the more appropriate expression μήτε ἀρχὴν
ζωῆς μήτε τέλος.

The most comprehensive nineteenth century theology of
Hebrews was set forth by Eduard K. A. Riehm (1830-88),[1] the
Halle OT scholar. A follower of Schleiermacher, Riehm occupied a mediating position between strictly orthodox interpreters and scholars with more pronounced rationalistic tendencies.

In a section devoted to Hebrews' use of the OT, Riehm
argues that the writer advanced a rigorously typical interpretation of the primitive narrative. In the mind of the
author Melchizedek was an authentic figure and Genesis was
a record of events which actually happened in the distant
antiquity.

> But Melchizedek as an historical person and the narra-
> tive which supplies the information about him as an his-
> torical event has no significance at all for the writer
> of Hebrews. Only that Scripture depicts him as a pic-
> ture of the NT priest-king does his person and the com-
> mentary on him acquire enduring import. . . . Thus the
> writer looks beyond the historical sense familiar to
> him and concerns himself with the enduring, ie, the NT
> significance of Melchizedek.

The Reformed theologian Eugene Ménégoz (1838-1921) was
a professor at the newly established Faculty of Protestant
Theology at the University of Paris. A leading proponent of
liberal Protestantism, Ménégoz was greatly influenced by
the critical symbolism of his Paris colleague, Auguste Saba-
tier. Ménégoz wrote his essay on Hebrews[2] in order to satisfy the need for a monograph on the theology of the Epistle
in French. While other biblical theologians propounded virtually a dogmatic theology of Hebrews, Ménégoz declares his
intention to expound only those doctrines which the author
himself regarded as of paramount importance, ie, the person
and priestly office of Christ.

Ménégoz's work is distinguished by the conviction that

---

1) *Der Lehrbegriff des Hebräerbriefes* (Basel & Ludwigsburg, 1867[2]).
2) *La théologie de l'Épître aux Hébreux* (Paris, 1894).

the religious philosophy of Philo exercised a pervasive influence upon the theology of Hebrews. The supposition that
the writer was a cultured Philonist converted to Christianity accounts for the Epistle being a synthesis of the Christian gospel and Jewish-Alexandrian theology. According to
Ménégoz, the Christology of Hebrews bears the unmistakable
stamp of the Logos doctrine of Philo. Hebrews' portrait of
Melchizedek as a type of the Son of God was borrowed from
Philo's understanding of Melchizedek as a manifestation of
the ethereal Logos. In the Philonic metaphysical schema, God
who is too elevated and pure to enter into immediate contact
with physical matter, employed a series of lesser intermedi-
aries to execute the divine will vis-à-vis the created world.
Hebrews borrowed from Philo's Logos the idea that the Son
of God was not a divine figure, but a created being of the
first rank.[1] Appeal is made to vs. 3 of our text for proof
that Christ is not coequal with God, but that he is an inferior celestial being. Thus ἀπάτωρ, ἀμήτωρ, κτλ teach that
like the first man Adam, the Son of God is the first of his
order of species. Anterior to time God the Father brought
the Son into existence via a special creative act.

> The metaphorical idea--difficult if not impossible to
> comprehend--of an eternal generation is alien to the
> author. One would be mistaken to take it in the abso-
> lute sense of an affirmation that the Son of God, even
> as Melchizedek, "has no beginning of his days" (vs. 3).
> These words only complete the preceding idea--"without
> father, without mother, without ancestor"--and they
> signify that the life of Christ did not commence with
> his birth. Christ was not born; he is the immediate and
> primordial product of the creative power of God.

Ménégoz sums up his explication of the person of the NT
high priest with the following observation:

> The Christology of our author is manifestly the attempt
> of a Philonic Christian who with his philosophical pre-
> mises seeks to render an account of the mysterious per-
> sonality of Christ. His conception of Christ is appre-
> ciably different from that of old orthodoxy. It relates

---

1) Thus Ménégoz asserts: "It is not a question here of the essential
divinity of Christ, of his deity, of his *homoöusia* with the Father. God
is one in the absolute sense. He is essentially distinct from the universe. He is beyond comparison. The Son, on the contrary, is not the
only one of his kind; he has 'companions,' 'fellow-creatures,' 'colleagues,' 'peers,' 'equals.'" *La théologie*, 84, 85.

more closely to the doctrine of the Arians than to that
of Athenasius. It has disappeared from the faith of the
Church through the ages and has been replaced by the
teaching of the essential divinity of Christ. . . .
Even in our day there are some theologians who understand it in the sense of the Christology of the Council
of Nicea. However, we do not believe that a careful
study of the text can lead to other conclusions than
those which we have just set forth.

(d) Roman Catholic Interpretation

Inasmuch as the Church assumed the role of authoritative
custodian of dogma, Roman Catholic interpretation was more
sheltered from the ebb and flow of radical criticism than
was Protestant exegesis. The majority of Catholic exegetes
countered the destructive criticism of the day by interpreting Scripture with one eye on the doctrines and pronounce-
ments of the Church. The importance of tradition is reflected in the numerous citations from the fathers. As one proponent of traditional Roman Catholic interpretation asserted,
"an exegesis without the Church, without respect for the
invariable judgments of the holy fathers and schoolmen is
subjectivism of the most serious sort."[1] But whereas main-
line Catholic interpretation reacted sharply against the
"naked rationalism" of the age which reduced the objective
truth of revelation to the level of arbitrary human wisdom,
a nucleus of Catholic interpreters were attracted to the
free spirit of the Enlightenment. Thus juxtaposed alongside
the predominant Roman Catholic conservatism was a stream of
Catholic neology which strove to modify traditional interpretation on the basis of modern scientific research. In the
main, nineteenth century Catholic exegetes continued to interpret the OT Melchizedek *Bild* via the classical *argumentum
e silentio* and to assert the eucharistic implications of
Melchizedek's "sacrifice" of bread and wine. On the other
hand, Catholic neologists generally discarded both the traditional argument from silence and the sacramental interpretation of Heb 7:1 ff.

---

1) Leonhard Zill, *Der Brief an die Hebräer* (Mainz, 1897), iv.

August Bisping (1811-84),[1] who appeals to the eucharistic
implications of the Melchizedek saga, stands in the main
stream of traditional Roman Catholic interpretation. By expounding the mysterious silence of Scripture in respect of
Melchizedek's life-data, Hebrews elevates the Salemite monarch as an elegant type of Christ, who is "without father as
man, without mother as God, without genealogy as high priest,
and without beginning and end of days as God's eternal Son."

The Roman Catholic fundamentalist Leonhard Zill (b. 1825)[2]
likewise reiterates traditional dogma by acknowledging Melchizedek's bread and wine "offering" as an ancient prefiguration of Christ's eucharistic sacrifice--"the most pre-
cious jewel of the Church." But whereas Moses attributed
primary importance to this proleptic sacrifice and secondary
importance to the blessing and the reception of tithes, the
writer of Hebrews reversed priorities by omitting mention
of the bread and wine sacrifice in keeping with his set purpose of demonstrating Melchizedek's superiority to the priests
of Levi. Zill's rigorous typological exegesis freely spiri-
tualizes the message of vs. 3. The negative and positive
statements of the text complement one another to affirm "the
independence and autonomy of the Melchizedekian order of
priesthood," which is inextricably rooted in the person of
the non-legal ministrant. Because Hebrews represents Melchizedek as a type of Christ wholly from the standpoint of
his appearance in Scripture, our text

> does not affirm the actual priestly continuance of Mel-
> chizedek either on earth or in heaven. . . . Melchiz-
> edek is in reality no more a priest for ever than he
> is without father and mother, without beginning and
> end of life.

Liborius Stengel (1801-33), who studied under the pro-
gressive Roman Catholic scholar J. L. Hug, was professor at
the Catholic Theological Seminary of the University of Freiburg, in Breisgau. Stengel, whose exposition of Hebrews was
set out in manuscript form,[3] was a Catholic neologist whose

---

1) *Erklärung des Briefes an die Hebräer* (Münster, 1854), 148 ff.
2) *Der Brief an die Hebräer übersetzt und erklärt* (Mainz, 1879),
300 ff.
3) *Erklärung des Briefes an die Hebräer* (Karlsruhe, 1849), 123 ff.

spirit of free and scientific inquiry ran counter to traditional Roman Catholic conservatism. The emergence of such
innovative and critical exegetes demonstrates that the spirit of independent scientific research promoted by the Enlightenment had not failed to penetrate Catholic interpretation, even though the resultant innovations were less far-
reaching than those advanced by Protestant neologists.
Stengel argues that biblical exegesis must be liberated from
the constricting shackles of ecclesiastical dogma. The modern school of scientific exegesis which had been rapidly
gaining momentum could not be held in check either by other-
worldly pietistic sentimentality or by arbitrary and inflex-
ible dogmatizing. Hence the message of the NT is not arrived
at by appeal to the judgments of the Church, but by an enlightened analysis of the text itself.[1]

At the very outset Stengel departs from traditional Catholic exegesis by affirming that the Melchizedek interpretation has not been constructed on the basis of a typology-
of-silence. The predicates of vs. 3 are to be interpreted
not in a figurative but in a strictly literal sense. Μήτε
ἀρχὴν ἡμερῶν κτλ refers not to the absence in Scripture of
the commencement and termination of Melchizedek's life or
priesthood, but it suggests features of an idealized supra-
human figure. Rather than propound various forced and arbitrary interpretations, it proves more satisfactory to pursue the following line of inquiry:

> Is it not entirely possible that the author was persuaded
> of the literal sense of the words which he penned? Could
> he not have held the rapturous opinion of Melchizedek
> that as "king of righteousness" and "king of peace" up-
> on the earth, he was a being of an entirely peculiar
> sort? Could he not have regarded him as one begotten
> apart from human parentage and without beginning and end
> of his life who, analogous to the Son of God, now con-
> tinues an eternal priest in the heavenlies?

Patently conditioned by critical conjectures of his day,

---

1) In the preface to his commentary, Stengel sets forth his conception of what happens when the Church becomes the sole guardian and interpreter of Scripture: "Then the highest truths upon which the salvation of men rests would be ostensibly the exclusive possession of the
'elect.' The Bible then would be for us human beings a closed book to
which the dogmatic theologians jealously guard the key."

Stengel speculates that the writer of Hebrews sketched his
portrait of Melchizedek from an opinion peculiar to himself,
or from an extant tradition which conceived of Melchizedek
as an idealized heavenly being. That Hebrews' conception of
Melchizedek was deduced from extra-biblical sources is reflected in Stengel's translation of vs. 8: "Ferner, hier
empfangen den Zehnten sterbliche Menschen, dort aber einer,
von dem gerühmt wird, dass er lebet." Thus it is clear that
Stengel freely ranges outside the bounds of traditional Roman Catholic exegesis and consistently draws inspiration
from the philosophical currency of his age.[1]

Aloys Schaeffer (1853-1914), who held academic posts at
Münster, Breslau and Strasbourg, undertook a commentary on
the whole of the NT. Although the work was never completed,
a commentary on Hebrews[2] appeared as the fifth volume in
the series. Schaeffer's NT commentaries were directed to the
pastor rather than to the scholar, but his explication of
the meaning and theological content of the biblical text has
commanded wide interest.

Schaeffer argues that the traditional Catholic position--
namely that not only what is recorded of Melchizedek, but
even more significantly what is *not* said about him constitutes the basis of the typological relationship--completely
misrepresents the intention of the author.

> After all, one must admit that the supposition that He-
> brews speaks of Melchizedek as a symbol who differs from
> the Aaronite priests not on the basis of what he is,
> but only on the basis of what he appears to be and that
> on the ground of the silence of the Genesis record, is
> more than doubtful. Without inflicting violence to the
> plain meaning of the text, how can one understand the
> terms ὅ ἐστιν (vs. 2) and ἔχων (vs. 3) other than as
> statements of what Melchizedek is and has? Consequently,
> that Hebrews promotes a typology-of-silence according
> to the methodology of Philo cannot be sustained from
> the text itself.

Schaeffer argues that Hebrews represents Melchizedek as a

---

1) Eg: "The author represents Melchizedek allegorically as the immortal *Menschengeist* united with God, who reigns royally over the souls of
men and who is able to lead men sacerdotally to union with God, the absolute *Geist*. This is precisely a description of Christ and what all
men should become through him." *Erklärung*, 131.

2) *Erklärung des Hebräerbriefes* (Münster, 1893), 185 ff.

type of Christ solely on the basis of (i) his act of blessing Abraham; and (ii) the interpretation of his name and
title[1] which later revelation identified as express characteristics of the coming Messiah. The writer thus conceived
of Melchizedek not as an historical personality, but pre-
eminently as a typical and idealized representation of the
NT priest-king.

The precise character of the symbolic relationship is un-
folded in greater detail. As the writer portrayed the reality (Christ) via an explication of the shadow (Melchizedek),
characteristics of the former were inevitably transferred
to the latter. This literary device was not restricted to
the writer of Hebrews. The prophet Isaiah, for example, in
describing Israel's deliverer from Babylonian captivity, ascribed to the human agent features of the divine Redeemer or
Servant of God blending, as it were, the two figures into
one. Thus the author of Hebrews contemplates

> the passing historic person of Melchizedek not in terms
> of his own individuality, but in his relationship to
> the Messiah, to the king of righteousness and peace. He
> regards him not merely as a contemporary of Abraham, but
> as one in whom Christ lives and is active. It was, in-
> deed, Melchizedek who blessed the patriarch. But because
> the first cause--the Messiah--unites with his instru-
> ment in an operation of this nature, a certain *communi-
> catio idiomatum* takes place. Thus something can be as-
> serted of Melchizedek who met Abraham, the complete re-
> ality of which is realized in the first cause--ie, in
> Christ--who is intimately bound up with him.

Thus for the author of Hebrews, Melchizedek functioned as
an "Organ" of the promised but now revealed Messiah, "who
animated him with his power in a fresh and supernatural way."

(e) Pietistic Interpretation

Nineteenth century interpretation in the pietistic tradition was an historical extension of the free, speculative

---

1) The author of Hebrews consciously omitted reference to Melchizedek's
bread and wine "sacrifice" (Gen 14:18) for the reason that the Aaronite
priests under the law brought their own meal offering and drink offering.
Mention of Melchizedek's prefiguration of the sacrifice of Christ would
have afforded no further evidence for the new order of priesthood.

approach to Scripture which arose a century earlier in reaction to naked rationalism and sterile orthodoxy. Although
wide variations within the movement existed, its interpreters
tended to be less concerned with critical problems, regarding
scientific theology as the husk rather than the kernel of
biblical studies. Interpretation in this tradition was frequently characterized by an attempt to unfold the deeper
spiritual truths seen to underlie the text via a vigorous
pneumatic exegesis. Thus spiritual receptivity rather than
historical or philological skills constitute the paramount
requisite for the interpreter of Scripture. In their quest
to extract pregnant spiritual meaning from the Bible, interpreters in the tradition here and there either disregard-
ed or overlooked the grammatico-historical sense of the text.
The occasional identification of Melchizedek with a preincarnate manifestation of the Son of God was justified via the
rationale that thereby greater honor would be attributed to
Christ and the Scriptures.

The Scottish Baptist clergyman Archibald McLean (1733-
1812)[1] judged that mere absence of recorded beginning and
end of life or priesthood would be insufficient ground for
ascribing Melchizedek with immortality. Hence in vs. 3 the
relative ὅς is supplied to give the reading, ". . . made
like to the Son of God, *who* abideth a priest continually."
Similarly, McLean argues that the writer effects a subtle
transition from Melchizedek to Christ when he affirms of
the latter, ὅτι ζῇ. As for the problem of Christ's involve-
ment in the patent historical event of the blessing and the
reception of the tithes from Abraham, McLean comments:

> Though it is true that Christ was not then a man, nor
> actually a priest, while he was typified and prophesied
> of under that character; yet, as the blessed effects
> of his priesthood reach backward to the entrance of
> sin, and forward to the end of time, and as he was in
> a peculiar manner represented by Melchizedek, so he
> might be said to bless and tithe Abraham by him as his
> most eminent type, both as a priest and in the order of
> his priesthood.

---

1) *A Paraphrase and Commentary on the Epistle to the Hebrews* (London,
1820[2]), repr. in *The Miscellaneous Works of Archibald McLean* (3 vols.;
London, 1847), I, 248 ff.

Karl August Auberlen (1824-64), professor of theology at
Basel and one of the leading representatives of Württemberg
pietism, developed in his essay on Hebrews 7[1] a highly spiritualized exegesis of our text. Auberlen's interpretation
is colored by his pneumatic concept of Scripture and by his
estimate of the far-reaching implications of the Psalm citation which is central to the argument of Heb 7:1 ff. As
for Hebrews' use of Psa 110:4 Auberlen remarks:

> The author squeezes nothing out of it, he inserts noth-
> ing into it, but he merely explains it. He simply dis-
> plays from the Psalm the deep things of the Spirit as
> they unfold to spiritual eyes. For a word from God in-
> deed contains something noteworthy, and inspiration con-
> sists not merely in the fact that one possesses the
> ability to write down Scripture, but also that one has
> the capacity to read Holy Scripture aright

Auberlen proceeds via a pneumatic exegesis to fathom the
depths of meaning inherent in the Messianic Genesis and
Psalm texts. Vss. 3 and 8 lie at the heart of his exegesis.
Rejecting the *argumentum e silentio* approach, Auberlen develops the thesis advanced by the fourth century monk Marcus
Eremitus. The negative statements of vs. 3 elevate Melchizedek above the Levites to a level of priesthood which is
dependent not upon any fleshly consideration but solely upon "Geist" and "Glauben," ie, entirely "on the basis of his
inner, spiritual relationship with God." The positive statements of vss. 3 and 8 constitute the principal resemblance
between the two priests. The Levitical priest (a paradigm
of dead works condemned by the law) was a carnal ministrant
who performed his ritual service apart from a living communion with God. However, Melchizedek, who stood in a viv-
ifying relation with the living God, rendered his priestly
service in spirit, truth and power. Thus the affirmation
that Melchizedek ζῆ implies that the one "who served the
living God in truth is precisely through this communion with
God removed from the power of death."[2] More specifically
Melchizedek, the living one, is an OT paradigm of the host

---

1) "Melchisedek's ewiges Leben und Priesterthum: Hebr. 7," *ThSK* (30,
1857), 453 ff.
2) Expressed otherwise, "The true priesthood is life and the true
life is priesthood."

of priest-kings of the New Covenant who minister before the throne of God day and night: "Melchizedek is thus an eternal priest in no other sense than according to the Apocalypse *all the blessed spirits are eternal priests*."

Adam Welch (1831-1902),[1] a conservative Scottish clergyman, also discounts the suggestion that Melchizedek was a type of Christ on the basis of the silence of the OT. The process of extracting from a mysterious primitive account certain *negative* notions and then translating these into far-reaching *positive* declarations via a process of "intellectual legerdemain" is contrary to the principles of sound reasoning and interpretation. As for the *argumentum e silentio,* Welch affirms: "This casuistical exposition, interpolated in the middle of a noble Epistle, is the fly which spoils the whole apothecary's ointment." If the eternal priesthood of Christ had been developed in the same manner, "it would rest on a foundation of sand." Concludes Welch: "Do men who use arguments of this kind never think how ridiculous they must appear in the eyes of infidels?"

The mysterious sayings about Melchizedek are clarified when one recognizes that ἔχων ("having") and ἀφωμοιωμένος ("resembling") are causal participles which explain *why* Melchizedek is denominated ἀπάτωρ, κτλ. The Salemite lacks parentage and genealogy precisely because he possesses neither beginning of days nor end of life. Similarly, μένει ἱερεὺς κτλ forcefully affirms that Melchizedek was, is and will continue a priest for ever. The conclusion drawn from such a literal and unadorned reading of the text is that "Melchizedek was an OT Christophany," one of the several preincarnate appearances of the Son of God.

---

1) *The Authorship of the Epistle to the Hebrews* (Edinburgh & London, 1898), 34 ff.

5. THE TWENTIETH CENTURY

(a) Protestant Interpretation

The inestimable nineteenth century contribution of a scientific grammatico-historical exegesis was augmented in the closing decade of that century by a quest for the *religionsgeschichtlich* derivation of the leading religious and theological concepts of the NT. Stimulated by the religio-historical researches of such scholars as Wilhelm Bousset (d. 1920), Richard Reitzenstein (d. 1931) and Hermann Gunkel (d. 1932), students of the NT began in earnest to look beyond the cradle of Christianity to the surrounding Hellenistic world for the genesis of the Bible's religious ideas. As a result of such efforts, interpretation during the present century (especially in Continental circles) has been dominated by the conviction that the NT represents the consummation of an evolutionary process of development from the primitive mythological motifs of extra-biblical religions. Interpreters who apply the comparative religions methodology to Heb 7:1 ff. variously suggest that Hebrews' priesthood Christology, in general, and the role of Melchizedek, in particular, may be attributed to apocalyptic, Philonic, Gnostic or Eastern Mystery sources. Melchizedek himself has been generally regarded as a mythological figure borrowed from extra-biblical literature. More conservative scholars, unconvinced that alleged Hellenistic sources are chronologically and logically antecedent to Hebrews, have redirected attention to the vast corpus of Jewish literature which undergirds the Epistle. Other interpreters have given a fresh interpretation of the first century document along traditional lines of a distinctively Christian revelation. In the light of mature research and reflection many of the theses which postulate dependence of Hebrews upon pagan mythological motifs have had to be revised. Nevertheless, twentieth century *religionsgeschichtlich* research has substantially enriched our understanding of motifs related to our Epistle which lie in the substrata of early Christianity.

Heinrich Weinel (1874-1936),[1] the Jena biblical theologian, argues that prior to the composition of Hebrews Melchizedek had been regarded as a sacred figure of a proto-Gnostic Jewish sect who made a fleeting visit to earth in human guise. Moreover, Alexandrian speculation represented by Philo conceived of Melchizedek as a manifestation of the high priestly Logos who leads the soul into experiences of divine intoxication. Against the backdrop of such religious motifs, the writer of Hebrews discovered Melchizedek embedded in the Jewish Law as a "silhouette of the Son of God." Thus in order to argue Melchizedek's non-legal priestly dignity, the writer characterized the Salemite as one possessing neither father and mother nor beginning and end of life. The remarkable feature of these deductions, insists Weinel, is that (following the method of Philo) they are constructed on the basis of the silence of the OT narrative! Weinel pointedly characterizes the extraordinary representation of Melchizedek in Heb 7:1 ff. as "a masterpiece of the peculiar biblical interpretation of that day."

Franz Josef Jérôme devotes a chapter in his monograph on the *Melchisedek-Bild* in Hebrews[2] to an exposition of vss. 1-4 of our text. Jérôme judges that since the Genesis 14 saga features one who appears as the ἐνσάρκωσις θεοῦ, it reads like "the resplendent page of a Book of Life."[3] However, the Psalmist and later the writer of Hebrews saw in this mysterious figure a remarkable outline of the Messianic priest who was to come.

Melchizedek is superior to Aaron because his priesthood is eternal. However, the eternity of the new order of priesthood is not fabricated on the traditional argument from silence, which as an interpretive method is no more than an "exegetical expediency." On the contrary, it rests squarely on the fact that Melchizedek is "the bearer of an undying priestly life founded entirely upon *inner spiritual grace*."

---

1) *Biblische Theologie des Neuen Testaments: Die Religion Jesu und des Urchristenthums* (Tübingen, 1928[4]).
2) *Das geschichtliche Melchisedek-Bild und seine Bedeutung in Hebräerbrief* (Freiburg, i.B., 1920), 73 ff.
3) Cf. Rev 22:19.

Jérôme's explication of Heb 7:1 ff. reflects this unifying theme.

> Melchizedek is without father and without mother because his priesthood is not founded upon the external circumstances of birth and descent. He is without beginning and end because his priesthood of grace is not bound by natural restrictions. He is made precisely like the Son of God, not in terms of any external relations, but owing to an abundant inner endowment of grace which qualifies him for priestly office. Such a *Gnaden-Priester* remains a priest for ever by virtue of what he is.

Thus Melchizedek has neither father nor mother as bearer of a supernatural office, for the supernatural principle of life is antithetical to all human and natural circumstances. In precisely this sense of the irrelevance of all human relations Jesus affirmed: "Anyone who does not hate his father and mother . . . cannot be my disciple"[1]; and again, "Who is my mother and my brothers?"[2] Similarly, a priest in whom the fullness of divine grace is operative, endowing him with its eternal character, of necessity "continues for ever." Thus whereas the decaying legal priesthood was characterized by "inward insufficiency" and "outward legality," the Melchizedekian order was a wholly interiorized priesthood of *grace* which death could not destroy. In short, Melchizedek is superior to Levi because the latter's priesthood lies in the sphere of law and nature, whereas the priesthood of Melchizedek is rooted in the realm of supernatural grace. Jérôme concludes that Heb 7:1-4 agrees remarkably with the law-grace dichotomy which Paul developed more formally in his other Epistles.

The question remains whether Melchizedek, the bearer of a priesthood which was supra-nature, was himself a supernatural being. Since the text states that Melchizedek was "gleichgemacht" to the Son of God (not merely "ähnlich"), the preceding must be answered in the affirmative. Ἀπάτωρ, ἀμήτωρ, κτλ thus depicts the supernatural side of the patently human priestly figure. Jérôme concludes that the Melchizedek of the Genesis saga, who participated directly in the fullness of the eternal being of God, may be regarded

---

1) Lk 14:26.
2) Matt 12:48.

as an incarnation of the *Urmensch* or Primal Man.

Alexander Nairne (1863-1936), professor of divinity at
Cambridge, advocated a Neoplatonic sacramental view of reality. His principal theological legacy was a mystical analysis of Hebrews under the title *The Epistle of Priesthood*,[1]
which one critic has assessed as one of the neglected theological works of modern times.[2] This thematic monograph was
supplemented by an exegetical commentary which appeared as
a volume in the Cambridge Greek Testament for Schools and
Colleges.[3]

If the argument of Heb 7:1 ff. appears "too scholastic,
. . . dry, half logical, half fanciful," it must be viewed
from the perspective of the Alexandrian Platonists to whom
it was written. Nairne argues that the whole concept of
priesthood developed in the Epistle is *sacramental* in character. Nairne's rich sacramental theology dominates his ho-
rizon: "When visual things reach out into the eternal and
carry us with them into God, there is a sacrament." The ultimate spiritual realities required by the Christian Platonist
addresses could only be apprehended by means of visual images
or symbols. Far from being detached one from the other, the
eternal reality is mystically present in the visual symbol.[4]
Thus Nairne suggests that one may proceed on "the reasonable
assurance of faith that all life is one, that the natural
is also divine." Expressed otherwise, "that which is *natural*
is *spiritual*."

To persuasively represent Christ's universal priesthood
the author searched the Scriptures for an appropriate symbol.

---

1) Edinburgh, 1915[2].
2) G.B. Caird, "Under-estimated Theological Books: Alexander Nairne's
'The Epistle of Priesthood,'" *ExpT* 72 (1961), 204-6. Unfettered by a
myriad of critical and exegetical details, *Epistle of Priesthood* sets
forth a wealth of insight and information via a deliberate contemplation
of the leading themes of the Epistle. As Caird suggests, "Like a connois-
seur in an antique shop he picks up his ideas like curios, passes them
lovingly from one hand to another, takes them to light, and puts them
back on the shelf until, all in good time, he is ready for a further,
closer look."
3) *The Epistle to the Hebrews*, CGTSC (Cambridge, 1917), 73 ff.
4) In Nairne's own poetic words, "the symbol trembles into unison
with the eternal truth of which it is the symbol."

> The high priest of this artificial order is Aaron. The
> High Priest of the other, real and living order is Jesus
> Christ. But cannot a name be found in the same sacred
> story which may stand as a type of Him, representing all
> the imperfect efforts of true priesthood which He in-
> spired and has now carried out to their inherent per-
> fection? . . . Will not Melchizedek serve this purpose?

In both the silences and the express affirmations of the OT

the author found justification for his thesis that Melchiz-

edek would be a "sacrament" of the eternal high priest "or-

dered in the course of divine and natural law with a kinship

which promises at last unity and consummation." The sketchy

account of the Salemite ministrant reads more like a legend

than a historical narrative. But the author was little con-

cerned with critical considerations; his interest was con-

sumed with the discovery in the sacred record of a non-legal

ministrant who bore an extraordinary similarity to the Son

of God. The resemblance between sacrament and reality is

sketched by the "daring epithets" of vs. 3.

> The lowly estate of Jesus in whom the divine Sonship was
> perfectly manifested, was righteous, peaceable, worthy
> of the tithe of homage from the seed of Abraham, yet how
> obscure. His royal descent might be "openly evident"
> (πρόδηλον) to those who owned him Lord; to Roman gover-
> nors and the Jewish aristocracy He was ἀπάτωρ, κτλ. And
> in μήτε ἀρχὴν ἡμερῶν κτλ it would be hardly fanciful to
> find a reminiscence of Isaiah 53 (LXX): "His judgment
> was taken away in being brought low. Who shall declare
> his generation? . . . Our soul shall see the long lived
> seed."

The clause μένει ἱερεὺς κτλ suggests that Melchizedek's

priesthood, operative in the world from earliest times, has

continued in force parallel to the priesthood of Levi. Far

from being extinguished by the latter, it outlasted the worn-

out legal order and presided over its demise. Melchizedek

fades from view only when, in the ongoing development of

priestly forms, he is replaced by Christ, the ultimate priest-

ly agent.

Nairne argues that throughout the course of history a

genuine priestly power has been operative. Its extension in-

to the realm of nature allows its designations as a "natural"

priesthood. From the very beginning of history this "priest-

ly instinct" in life has been progressively evolving from

rudimentary to more highly developed forms. Nairne does not

hesitate to characterize this development of natural and
universal priestly forms as a process of evolution. Thus
Melchizedek is cited as a significant representative in the
evolutionary development of the natural priesthood over the
whole of life. But the sacramental principle which affirms
that "what is natural is spiritual," leads to the supposition
that this natural and universal priesthood should consumate
in an ultimate priestly form. Hence Nairne concludes that
"the priesthood of our Lord Jesus Christ is the fulfillment
of the natural and universal priesthood of the ancient world."
In contemporary language, priesthood "after the order of Melchizedek" would be characterized as a "natural priesthood."

A history of interpretation of a NT text would be incomplete without reference to the renowned commentary of Strack-
Billerbeck.[1] Professor of Oriental languages and founder of
the *Institutum Judaicum* during his lengthy career at Berlin,
Hermann Strack (1848-1922) was one of the leading rabbinic
scholars of his generation. Paul Billerbeck (1853-1932), on
the other hand, was a pastor rather than an academic theologian. Nevertheless, Billerbeck devoted much of his life
to the actual preparation of the *Kommentar*, whereas Strack
assumed editorial responsibility for the work. Building on
the foundations laid by such predecessors as John Lightfoot
(1699), Christian Schöttgen (1751) and J. J. Wettstein (1754),
Strack-Billerbeck have gathered under selected NT texts a
wealth of rabbinic material which illustrates the faith of
the Jews during the early centuries of the Christian church.
Fortunately the work sets aside the rabbinic consensus when
it contravenes the patent sense of the NT.[2] But lest one be
led into false exegesis, discretion must be exercised when
seeking to elucidate the NT in the light of supposed 'paral-

---

1) *Kommentar zum Neuen Testament aus Talmud und Midrasch* (4 vols.;
München, 1922-28), III, 692 ff.

2) Eg, on Heb 7:7. Thus the criticism of some scholars against the
work appears unduly severe. Note, eg, V. Burch's estimate of Strack-
Billerbeck's treatment of Hebrews: "The Epistle was sunk in an ocean of
Jewish literature. Not a single passage had a chance of coming to the
surface as a Christian statement against a load of parallels from Talmud and Targum. Its author became more hebraic than Moses." *The Epistle
to the Hebrews: Its Sources and Message* (London, 1936), 12.

lels' from the complex of late Jewish literature.[1]

Strack-Billerbeck recognize the crucial significance of
vs. 3 to the interpretation of our text. On the basis of
various Jewish sources ἀπάτωρ, ἀμήτωρ could denote either
(i) one whose mother and father are deceased, (ii) one whose
parents are unknown, as in the case of a foundling child,
or (iii) one whose genealogical register is lacking. Evidence from the OT and rabbinic Judaism suggests that Melchizedek was designated thus because he failed to satisfy
the prescribed requirements for accession to Levitical priesthood. Ezra 2:61-63 and Neh 7:63-65 are adduced as proof that
aspirants unable to demonstrate Aaronic descent from the
genealogical registers were rejected as unfit for service in
the sanctuary. The rabbis amplified the OT prescription that
a priest take only a pure Israelite to wife by further insisting, in the case of a priest who sought to marry a woman
of Aaronic descent, that the prospective bride certify her
ancestry through the four preceding generations. In the case
of a daughter of a Levite or a common Israelite, ancestry
through a fifth generation had to be verified.[2] The issue
of demonstrable priestly descent was such a weighty issue
with the Jews that the great Sanhedrin was convened to exam-
ine claims to priestly or Levitical status.[3] According to
Josephus, a diaspora Jew who aspired to priesthood in a foreign land was obliged to dispatch to Jerusalem for examination by the authorities a certified record of his priestly
ancestry.[4] Μήτε ἀρχὴν ἡμερῶν κτλ is likewise interpreted on
the basis of the silence of Genesis. Underlying the phrase
is the succinct rabbinic axiom: "quod non in thora non in
mundo." The rabbis, for example, believed that since no mention of warfare is recorded in Scripture previous to the
battle between the forces of king Amraphel and king Bera,
the contest recorded in Genesis 14 was the first incident
of warfare to have occurred in history.[5]

---

1) See especially in this regard, Otto Michel, in *Studies on the
Jewish Background of the New Testament* (Assen, 1969), 2.
2) M. Kidd. 4:4 ff.
3) M. Midd. 5:4.
4) *Contra Apionem* I. 7.
5) Tanch. B. לך לך (32b).

Strack-Billerbeck's identification with rabbinic hermeneutics clearly emerges in their explication of μένει ἱερεὺς κτλ. The declaration that Melchizedek "continues a priest for ever" was deduced by the author from the oracle of Psa 110:4. Hebrews' transference to Melchizedek of an affirmation directed to Christ was in accord with the גזרה שוה ("inference by analogy"), one of the seven rules of Hillel for interpreting the Talmud and Midrashim. Since the Messiah is designated כהן לעולם, and Melchizedek "has neither beginning of days nor end of life," the author concluded by inference that the Salemite likewise "continues a priest for ever."[1]

Adolf Schlatter (1852-1938), the Swiss biblical interpreter, historian and theologian, held academic posts at Berne, Berlin and Tübingen. A respected scholar who conformed to no contemporary theological 'school,' Schlatter avoided both the neatly devised formulae of the traditional dogmatists and the reduction of biblical doctrine by rationalistic theologians. In his view biblical theology ought not to be restricted to abstract theorizing, but should focus on the exposition of the Word of God and the evoking of an outworking faith. Schlatter's extensive writings in the areas of biblical exegesis, theology and history have become of late the object of renewed interest and attention.[2] His principal legacy is a commentary on the entire NT[3] written primarily for the non-technical reader.

Schlatter argues that Hebrews was directed to a group of Jewish-Christians from whom external separation from the ritual cultus was made difficult by a Gnostic idealization of Judaism. Hebrews' skillful explication of the priesthood of Melchizedek suggests that the Gnosticizers sought to abolish the distinction between the OT revelation and Jesus by appeal to current mystical speculation about Melchizedek. The Gnosticizers argued that followers of Jesus need not renounce

---

1) Cf H. Strack, *Einleitung in Talmud und Midrasch* (München, 1921[5]), 97
2) Note especially two recent monographs on Schlatter: A. Bailer, *Das systematische Prinzip der Theologie A. Schlatters* (Stuttgart, 1968). G. Egg, *Adolf Schlatters kritische Position* (Stuttgart, 1968).
3) *Erläuterungen zum Neuen Testament* (3 vols.; Stuttgart, 1928[4]). Heb 7:1 ff. appears in vol. III, 328 ff.

Judaism since from earliest times the OT laid claim to a
priesthood whose dignity was likewise predicated upon the
non-existence of human parentage.[1] To counter Gnostic mythical speculation about Melchizedek the writer of Hebrews
advanced his own interpretation of the ancient figure based
on the silences of the Genesis 14 narrative and the positive
declaration of Psa 110:4. Thus Schlatter argues that when
Melchizedek approached the sacred altar he had no need to
submit to a succession of queries as did the Levitical priests.

> What is the name of your father? Did he come from the
> family of Aaron? What is the name of your mother? Was
> she a pure virgin of Israel in accord with the law? Where
> is your genealogical register? Can you prove beyond doubt
> that your priestly descent is uninterrupted?

If the issue of greatest moment is the perpetuity ascribed
by the Psalmist to the new priestly order, in what sense is
Melchizedek's priesthood eternal? The Gnostic teachers appealed to mythical legends which depicted Melchizedek as a
heavenly figure who made a fleeting appearance to earth in
human guise. Schlatter turns to Scripture, the final arbiter,
and finds no support for such presumption. "Three men are
compared with one another: Aaron, Melchizedek, and Jesus.
Between Aaron, the man, and Jesus, who like ourselves assumed flesh and blood, we certainly do not find Melchizedek
the angel." The issue reduces to the efficacy of the historical Melchizedek in relation to the ongoing course of human
history. The solution to the problem lies in a later statement of the Epistle to the effect that, although Abel expired
long ago, the power of his blood sacrificed continues to
speak.[2] Whenever injustice occurs, the blood of Abel cries
out to God from the earth. In precisely this sense may Melchizedek's priesthood be regarded as a perpetual ministration. In the distant past Melchizedek blessed the patriarch,
ministering to him in the name of God Most High. That ancient
priestly service has remained efficacious through the suc-
ceeding centuries of time.

> The Psalm text shows that his priesthood has not been
> forgotten before God, but that it is a present reality.

---

1) *Die Theologie der Apostel* (Stuttgart, 1922), 461.
2) Heb 11:4.

> Consequently, it possesses a continuing efficacy and
> validity. What occurs on earth according to divine dis-
> position takes place in time, but does not vanish with
> time. As the future is bound with the present in the
> sight and will of God, so that vanishes not which was
> accomplished through God and for him. It reaches down
> to the present and does not pass away, but sustains it-
> self with enduring effect.

Since God added his "amen" to the Salemite's ancient priestly service, Schlatter concludes that Melchizedek even now
stands before God endowed with a priestly dignity which is
imperishable.

Hans Windisch (1881-1935) was professor of NT at Leiden,
Kiel and Halle. A leading proponent of the *religionsgeschichtlich* method, Windisch wrote numerous monographs on the relationship of primitive Christianity to contemporary Near Eastern religions. His Hebrews commentary[1] was the first major
exposition of the Epistle from the perspective of the twentieth century history of religions school.

Windisch argues that in Heb 7:1 ff., Psa 110:4 and Gen
14:17-20 are succinctly summarized and, with one eye on Jesus
the Messiah, "conclusions are drawn by the author of Hebrews
which the biblical writers never had in mind." In an excursus which gives detailed consideration to the *religionsgeschichtlich* aspects of the Melchizedek speculation, Windisch
affirms that "according to Heb 7:1-4, the one who encountered
Abraham was no ordinary human figure but a divine being in
human form, who was employed precisely as a 'double' and
forerunner of Jesus the Son of God." Thus ἀπάτωρ, ἀμήτωρ
are to be understood in the strictly literal sense of his
mysterious, supra-human origin.[2] Particular significance is
attributed to the fact that these terms were employed in the
Hellenistic world as attributes of the gods.[3] The third mem-

---

1) *Der Hebräerbrief*, HNT 14 (Tübingen, 1931[2]), 59 ff.

2) Cf Walter Bauer (1877-1960), the renowned Göttingen lexicographer,
who suggests that Melchizedek's description as ἀπάτωρ, κτλ points to the
miraculous heavenly origin of the supra-human (angel?) being who mysteriously appeared in the patriarchal history. Thus understood, it readily
follows that "Jesus was a high priest *just like Melchizedek*" (Psa 110:
4). *Griechisch-Deutches Wörterbuch zu den Schriften des NT* (Berlin, 1949-
52[4]), 91, 163, 1591.

3) Pollox, *Onom.* III. 26. Cf Philo, *De op. mund.* 100. Cf also an
Egyptian hymn to Putah: "You have no father who has begotten you when
you were formed; you have no mother who has borne you."

ber of the triad, ἀγενεαλόγητος, is best explained in the
light of the Philonic text which affirms that God himself
was the father of the λόγος θεῖος and that σοφία was his
mother.[1] The unbounded duration of Melchizedek's life, μήτε
ζωῆς τέλος, follows from the myth that he never succumbed to
death, but that he was miraculously removed from earth like
Enoch the ante-deluvian saint.[2] The correspondence established between Melchizedek and the Son of God can be traced
to the Philonic belief that both figures are manifestations
of the priestly Logos and hence are similar to one another.[3]
Finally, the myth depicts Melchizedek as a heavenly being
who ministers in the presence of God throughout eternity.

Melchizedek is depicted in vs. 3 as a heavenly priest
invested with extraordinary dignity. He is the prototype in
relation to whom Jesus, the copy, would appear superfluous.
The fact that Melchizedek bears no direct relevance to the
religious needs of men and that in the latter half of the
chapter he retires completely from view, suggests that the
author has incorporated a strand of Melchizedek speculation
foreign to the thought-world of Scripture. The source from
which Hebrews borrowed its conception of Melchizedek is a
matter of considerable interest to Windisch. Although Hebrews' development of the Melchizedek motif bears a striking
resemblance to the Philonic Logos, who as high priest im-
parts righteousness and peace to the souls of men, the Alexandrian knows nothing of an incarnation of the Logos. Thus
Windisch judges that the author derived his conception of
the incarnate heavenly figure from apocalyptic Enoch speculation reflected in the Slavonic Book of Enoch and the so-
called "Mandean" III Enoch.[4] Concludes Windisch: "In these
verses a piece of 'Schriftgnosis' is furnished which does
not stand in complete harmony with the rest of the teachings
of Hebrews and which is scarcely of Christian origin."

---

1) De fug. 109. Cf De Abr. 31.
2) Gen 5:24.
3) Cf Leg. alleg. III. 82 with De confus. ling. 63, 146.
4) Windisch alleges that the "Mandean" writings shed considerable
light upon Hebrews. Primitive Oriental Gnosticism which underlay the
Mandean religion blended with Jewish Gnosticism to yield a Christian
Gnosis which accounts for much of the mysticism in Heb 7:1 ff.

James Moffatt (1870-1944), renowned biblical exegete,
historian and Bible translator held academic posts at Mans-
field College, Oxford, the United Free Church college, Glas-
gow, and Union Theological Seminary, New York. In his Hebrews commentary in the ICC,[1] Moffatt expounds Heb 7:1 ff.
from the perspective of the metaphysical schema of Philo:
"The fanciful argument from the priesthood of Melchizedek--
fanciful to us, but forceful then--swings from this conception." If the *religionsgeschichtlich* problem can be reduced
to the basic question, "to Hebraize or Hellenize?"[2] clearly
Moffatt views our text through the spectacles of the Hellenistic world.

Heb 7:1-3 is regarded as a compact sermon on Gen 14:17
ff., "the fantastic interpretation of the Melchizedek epi-
sode" being a creation of the author himself. Philo's hermeneutic affords a clue to Hebrews' allegorical exposition
of the OT. Philo not only thought of Melchizedek in terms
of "the peaceful, persuasive influence of a really royal
mind," but he proceeded on the Alexandrian principle that
what is not expressly recorded bears no ultimate reality.[3]
The epithets ἀπάτωρ and ἀμήτωρ are "boldly lifted from their
pagan associations" to emphasize that Melchizedek had no
generic link with the visible order of things. "Without father and mother"!

> The phrase is no more than a fanciful deduction from the
> wording or rather the silence of the legend, just as the
> original priest-king Gudea says to the goddess in the
> Sumerian tale, "I have no mother, thou art my mother; I
> have no father, thou art my father."

Although Melchizedek is a prototype of Christ, Moffatt re-
fuses to concede that ἀπάτωρ, ἀμήτωρ convey ontological
truths about the Son of God. What then is affirmed by the
negative predicates of vs. 3?

> Reading the record in the light of Psa 110:4, and on the
> Alexandrian principle that the very silence of Scripture

---

1) *A Critical and Exegetical Commentary on the Epistle to the Hebrews,*
ICC (Edinburgh, 1924), 90 ff.
2) V. Burch: "To Hebraize or to Hellenize, that is the question of
questions for the interpretation of the Epistle to the Hebrews." *The
Epistle to the Hebrews: Its Sources and Message* (London, 1936), 3.
3) *De ebr.* 14; *Quod det.* 48.

is charged with meaning, the writer divines in Melchizedek a priest who is permanent.

According to Jean Héring,[1] of the University of Strasbourg, the writer's "curious argument" about Melchizedek in Heb 7: 3 is far from clear. The tantalizing question of the mortality or immortality of Melchizedek is obscured by the author's consuming interest in the eternity of Christ: "Apparently typology here slips into allegory. What is said of Melchizedek really refers to Christ."

The underlying obscurity reappears in vs. 8 with the further reference to the immortality of the Canaanite king.

There again no precise information is given about the import of that life. Could he have been transported to heaven like Enoch and Elijah? Might he be an appearance of Christ? We cannot be sure.

Héring observes that the idea of an actual incarnation of a type of Christ was not unknown in the apostolic community. Did not the apostle Paul himself insist that the rock in the desert was both a figure of Christ and Christ himself?[2]

Ersnt Käsemann (b. 1906) fulfilled a distinguished academic career as professor of NT at Mainz, Göttingen, and Tübingen. His contribution to the literature of Hebrews is a provocative essay dealing with the *religionsgeschichtlich* background of the Epistle under the motif of the wandering people of God in quest of their heavenly home.[3] Its investigation of the evolution of thought from primitive mythical (ie, Gnostic) elements represents the definitive interpretation of the Epistle from the perspective of a comparative religions methodology. Käsemann insists that a careful examination of Hebrews will reveal that early Christian preachers did not hesitate to employ extra-biblical mythical conceptions in the proclamation of the gospel. Specifically, Hebrews' priesthood Christology was constructed by extensive appeal to early Gnostic mythical traditions. The situation could not have been otherwise, for when the early Christian movement expanded beyond Palestinian soil into the Hellenis-

---

1) *L'Épître aux Hébreux*, Commentaire du Nouveau Testament XII (Neuchatel & Paris, 1954), 65 ff.

2) I Cor 10:4.

3) *Das wandernde Gottesvolk: Eine Untersuchung zum Hebräerbrief* (Göttingen, 1961[4]).

tic world it quickly assimilated elements of Gnostic mysticism.

Käsemann seeks to isolate more precisely those primitive
traditions underlying the author's explication of the priesthood of Melchizedek and of Christ in Heb 7:1 ff. Käsemann
counters the argument that the transference of the high
priestly motif to the Son of God was an original creation of
Hebrews. The fact that the motif of Christ as heavenly high
priest in the Clementine and Ignatian correspondence[1] cannot be explained on the basis of dependence upon Hebrews
alone, argues for the existence of an earlier liturgical
tradition which itself arose from still earlier mythical traditions. As other interpreters have observed, Hebrews' high
priesthood Christology reflects a striking likeness to the
Philonic λόγος-ἀρχιερεύς motif. But since Philo's high priest
is a cosmological rather than a soteriological figure, dependence of Hebrews upon the Alexandrian philosopher is discounted. The thesis that both Hebrews and Philo borrowed the
tradition of the heavenly high priest from a common religious-
philosophical substratum is advanced as a more probable explanation of the parallels which exist in the two writings.
In this regard Käsemann argues that a striking correspondence
is apparent between the Philonic λόγος-ἀρχιερεύς idea and
certain late Jewish mythological motifs. Thus the archangel
Michael is represented in Jewish apocalyptic literature as
a high priestly ministrant who guides the souls of the righteous to the heavenly Jerusalem and there pleads their cause
before the Holy One. Furthermore, it can be shown that *Eli-
jah-Phinehas* was not only acclaimed a legal high priest of
the Messianic age,[2] but also that he was regarded as an incarnation of the "Urmensch-Erlöser" according to Jewish apocalyptic expectation. In addition, late Jewish mysticism depicts *Metatron* as an apocalyptic figure who performs a complex of functions in the heavenly realm. As the heavenly
"Intercessor, Intermediary and Advocate,"[3] Metatron is con-

---

1) I Clem. 36:1; 61:3; 64:1. Ignatius, *Philad.* 9:1.
2) Mal 3:1; 2:4; Numb 25:7, 13. Cf Strack-Billerbeck, *Kommentar*, IV,
462 ff.
3) See Hugo Odeberg, *III Enoch* (Cambridge, 1928), 115.

sistently denoted as the "Prince of the Presence"[1] as well
as the first of God's creation, or the Primal Man.[2] Finally,
in the various Adam writings *Melchizedek* himself is regarded
as yet another incarnation of the Primal Man. Thus Käsemann
remarks:

> Melchizedek, who is denoted as great high priest, dis-
> charges his office at the middle point on earth and is
> then buried there, as the same is true of Adam accord-
> ing to ancient speculations. In the Christian *Book of
> Adam in the East*, this is represented in such a way that
> Melchizedek ministers at the grave of Adam, bears the
> body of Adam to the hill of Calvary and is thus the
> link between the high priest Adam and Christ the third
> high priest.

Thus Käsemann argues that in late Jewish and early Christian
Gnostic thought, "Messianic high priest" was a title attributed to the Primal Man who was identified with a range of
historical and mythical figures from earliest times. Where-
upon:

> *Melchizedek* can be regarded as an incarnation of the Pri-
> mal Man and to that extent a bearer of the Messianic
> high priestly dignity, as elsewhere Moses, Elijah-Phine-
> has, Metatron, Shem or Michael. . . . The figures change,
> but the pattern remains the same.

Käsemann argues that Hebrews (likewise Philo) developed
the idea of the priesthood of Melchizedek from these same
Gnostic traditions. The predicates descriptive of Melchizedek in vss. 2 ff. could not have been derived from Genesis
14 and Psalm 110 alone. Hence attempts to prove that Melchizedek was an eternal heavenly being based on the absence
of recorded life-data are misguided. Moreover, the attributes
of vss. 2, 3 and 8 bear striking resemblance to those which
the Gnostic Anthropos Myth ascribed to an *aeon*. How does one
account for the fact that the Philonic *argumentum e silentio*
and Käsemann's appeal to the Gnostic aeon yield the identical result of a supra-mundane, eternal priest? Our interpreter both poses the problem and advances his own solution.

> Is this accidental? One may deny this on the basis of
> Hebrews' very precise knowledge of Gnosis and hereby con-
> firm the fact that Philo's Melchizedek speculation is
> that of a specific Jewish-Gnostic tradition.

---

1) III Enoch 3:1, 9:1, etc.
2) See III Enoch 48 C1; Odeberg, 164.

The commentary[1] of Otto Michel (b. 1903), former professor of NT and late Judaism and director of the *Institutum
Judaicum* at Tübingen, has more than doubled in size while
passing through six editions over a period of thirty years.
By virtue of its high standard of philological, theological
and *religionsgeschichtlich* research, Michel's work may be
judged the outstanding German language commentary on Hebrews
published in the twentieth century. Clearly Michel's exegetical results have been arrived at only after the most patient
reflection on the biblical text. One also respects the manner in which, when confronted with a difficulty which resists
clarification, Michel poses the problem in the form of a
question with perhaps a suggestion as to a likely line of
approach.

Heb 7:1 ff. expounds "the esoteric mystery of the priesthood of Christ" implicit in the oracle of Psalm 110. Melchizedek is exhibited as the initial member of an eschatological
order which has culminated in the high priest of the New
Covenant. A debated issue is whether Hebrews' interpretation
of Melchizedek was derived from the Genesis and Psalm texts,
or whether extant Gnostic mythical traditions were recast.
Michel cautiously notes that some association with the Gnostic "Urmensch" myth might be supposed because of Adam's role
therein as a high priest. Nevertheless, the probable source
of the Melchizedek interpretation is the OT itself. Via a
form-critical analysis of vss. 1-3 Michel suggests that the
declaration of the Psalmist was reinforced by a midrashic
exegesis of the Genesis text which the author of Hebrews recast in a Hellenistic form: "Gen 14:17-20 is cited, para-
phrased, and interpreted according to the model of a Jewish-
rabbinic Midrash." Hebrews' exegesis is analogous to that
of 4Q Florilegium, wherein an antecedent revelation is regarded as the pledge of a future, eschatological fulfillment. In Heb 7:1-3 the writer employed just such a combination of two OT texts, the later (Psa 110:4) confirming the

---

1) *Der Brief an die Hebräer*, MK 13 (Göttingen, 1966[12]), 255 ff. The
first four editions of the series were prepared by Gottlieb Lünemann
(1855 ff.), the fifth and sixth editions by Berhard Weiss (1888 ff.).

hidden eschatological implications of the earlier (Gen 14: 17 ff.).

Vs. 3 is regarded as a brief poem of four strophes, the purpose of which is to extol Melchizedek as an eschatological type of Christ. Of the numerous interpretations advanced in respect of the alpha-privative triad ἀπάτωρ, κτλ only two merit serious consideration: (i) the essentially Jewish notion that Melchizedek was begotten from no legitimate priestly line, and (ii) the Hellenistic mythological concept of a supra-human figure endowed with a mysterious heavenly origin. Here a characteristic tantalizing question is posed: "Does the first line of our poem stress Melchizedek's scandalous relation to the law, or does it lead into oriental mythology and symbolism?" The third term of the triad argues for the non-mythological view that "Melchizedek had no legitimate pedigree." The second line of the hymn, μήτε ἀρχὴν ἡμερῶν κτλ, suggests that from the perspective of Scripture, the life and activity of this non-Levitical priest had no bounds whatever. The following line of the poetic piece, ἀφωμοιωμένος κτλ, transfers the preceding statements about the ancient "Abbild" to the Messianic "Urbild." The events in the primitive history (principally the combination of royalty and priesthood in a nonperishable, non-Aaronic ministrant) were divinely ordained symbols of an eschatological reality which found fulfillment in Christ. The final line of the traditional material, μένει ἱερεὺς κτλ, transcends the warrant of the underlying OT texts by endowing Melchizedek with a perpetual priesthood. Thus the "Bleiben" of the non-legal ministrant is rich in eschatological significance. A postscript to the preceding poem--ie, the deduction from Psa 110:4 that Melchizedek "lives on"--suggests that Scripture with all its authority certifies that "God has given Melchizedek a share in his very own life."

F. F. Bruce (b. 1910), currently Rylands Professor of Biblical Criticism and Exegesis at the University of Manchester, published an exposition of Hebrews in the New International Commentary series.[1] Bruce's exegesis is characterized by a

---

1) *The Epistle to the Hebrews*, NIC (London & Edinburgh, 1965), 133 ff.

reluctance to affirm any more or less than a careful grammatical, philological and historical analysis of the text warrants.

Bruce observes Hebrews' high regard for Scripture, commenting: "To our author the OT is a divine oracle from first to last." The writer viewed the ancient Scriptures as "a parable or mystery" which waits for explication by an enlightened interpreter. The hermeneutical method of Hebrews is thus not unlike the *rāz-pesher* schema of OT apocalyptic and non-conformist Jewish exegesis.[1]

The typological statements of vs. 3 are derived from the Genesis text via an argument from silence widely employed by both Philo and the later synagogue. Hence vs. 3 cannot be understood in a literal sense, as if to suggest that Melchizedek was "a biological anomaly, or an angel in human guize." Rather Melchizedek is depicted as one devoid of parentage and genealogy since (by divine superintendence) no mention is made in the Genesis record of parentage or ancestry. To this Bruce adds the instructive remark:

> Historically Melchizedek appears to have belonged to a dynasty of priest-kings in which he had both predecessors and successors. If this point had been put to our author, he would have agreed at once, no doubt; but this consideration was foreign to his purpose. The important consideration was the account of Melchizedek in holy writ.

By so designating Melchizedek as one whose parentage and family tree are nonexistent (in Scripture), the author may have also sought to differentiate the latter from the Aaronic ministrants who as late as the Maccabean era were disqualified from service if descent from the legitimate priestly line could not be proven. Moreover the typical figure is "made like unto the Son of God" both in respect of the positive declarations of Scripture and the absence of data as to parentage, descent, beginning and cessation of life. Bruce carefully avoids the dilemma of many earlier exegetes who sought a precise application of each of the preceding predicates to Christ. The statements of vs. 3 are to be applied

---

1) Cf F.F. Bruce, *Biblical Exegesis in the Qumran Texts* (London, 1960), 7 ff., 75 ff.

to the antitype in accord with the following principle:

> It is the eternal being of the Son of God that is here
> in view; not his human life. Our author has no docetic
> view of Christ; . . . But in his eternal being the Son
> of God has really, as Melchizedek has typically, "neither
> beginning of days nor end of life."

(b) Roman Catholic Interpretation

Because of the greater significance of tradition and authority, twentieth century Roman Catholic interpretation of
Heb 7:1 ff. is less dominated by radical theories of *religionsgeschichtlich* research than is Protestant exegesis.
Catholic exegetes have been generally content to trace linguistic parallels in the writings of Philo; Gnostic and other
Eastern Mystery motifs are cited with more or less detached
interest. The typological argument based on the silence of
the OT remains a popular approach and explication of the
higher spiritual meaning of the text, in accord with the
Catholic *sensus plenior*, is not entirely wanting. Modern
Catholic interpretation has progressed far from earlier scholastic exegesis which was largely preoccupied with the alleged eucharistic implications of the Melchizedek saga.[1] The
disparity between Protestant and Roman Catholic interpretation of our text has been largely eliminated by mutual ad-
herence to a scientific grammatico-historical method.

Julius Graf (b. 1878), who received a doctorate from the
Catholic Theological Faculty of the University of Tübingen,
lectured at the *Realgymnasium* at Gmünd in Swabia. Although
relatively unknown, Graf's commentary on Hebrews[2] ranks among
the best Catholic commentaries of the first half of the century. The reader quickly discovers that Graf has written an
exposition of the Epistle which, by virtue of the richness
of its imagery, is highly stimulating and suggestive.

---

1) Nevertheless, commitment to the traditional eucharistic interpretation has not died out altogether. Referring to the precise manner in
which Melchizedek foreshadowed the priesthood of Christ, Ignaz Rohr
comments: "The prefiguration can be in the offering of bread and wine."
Der Hebräerbrief, Die Heilige Schrift des Neuen Testaments 10 (Bonn,
1932[4]), 37.

2) *Der Hebräerbrief: wissenschaftlich-praktische Erklärung* (Freiburg,
i.B., 1918), 137 ff.

In order to grasp the message of Hebrews, Graf argues,
one need not journey to Alexandria and there immerse one's
self in Philo. Instead, attention should be paid to the exegetical method of the rabbinical academies in Palestine,
where by ingenious explanations and clever subtleties the
hidden meaning of the law was expounded. Graf judges that
the patently historical OT Melchizedek account was mystically expounded in Hebrews. Thus although the author's starting point was the narrative of Gen 14:18 ff., "the portrait
of Melchizedek soars far above the OT and the old religion,
for it is the portrait of an everlasting priest." By virtue
of his intimate prophetic relationship to Jesus, "wonder
upon wonder are heaped upon the person of Melchizedek."

> Everything about him is mystery: he is no tangible hu-
> man being as we, the first hour of whose life is al-
> ready clear. . . . He is a superhuman figure, by no means
> as human as we when one pays full regard to the ground
> of his existence. A mysterious twilight surrounds his
> person; a heavenly twilight envelopes him from above.
> He is a stranger surrounded with mysterious glory; on
> the other hand, he is an eminent figure who parades with
> solemn and majestic gait.

The mysterious origin of this ancient priest-king, his in-
compatibility with the legal priesthood, and the unbounded
expanse of his life are signified by the epithets of vs. 3.
Scripture leaves us in the dark as to his origin; we know
nothing whatever about his father, mother, or family tree.
Genesis sheds no light on the facts of his historical existence: When was he born? When did he die? From these extraordinary circumstances Graf concludes: "In this silence of the
Scripture resides a divine plan and a divine mystery. Everything in his life is symbolic of the great Messianic future."

Ignaz Rohr,[1] professor of theology at the Catholic Faculty at Tübingen, judges that Melchizedek's prefiguration
of Christ could be founded either on his ancient offering of
bread and wine, or on the eternity ascribed to his priesthood. The peculiar "silence of the Holy Scriptures as to
Melchizedek's family tree should not be taken as proof that
he was a celestial being from all eternity which suddenly

---

1) *Der Hebräerbrief* (Bonn, 1932[4]), 30 ff.

flashed across the world's scene like a brilliant meteor only
to vanish again." By sketching such a portrait from the silences of the OT and applying the results to Christ, the author has reproduced a classic "piece of Alexandrian and rabbinic argumentation."

Ceslaus Spicq (b. 1901) was professor of NT at the French
Dominican faculty at Le Saulchoir and at the University of
Fribourg in Switzerland. In Spicq's two-volume critical commentary on Hebrews[1] leading issues of introduction are dis-
cussed in great detail in fourteen chapters. Of particular
relevance to the present study are chapters on the relationship of Hebrews to Philo, the theology of the Epistle, and
the author's use of the OT. A valuable chapter is devoted
to a comprehensive (albeit not exhaustive) annotated bibli-
ography of Hebrews from the patristic era to 1950. Volume
two features a detailed analysis of the text, richly supplemented by eleven valuable excurses on selected themes.
By virtue of its wealth of background material and its in-
cisive linguistic and theological analysis, Spicq's commentary represents the most significant twentieth century Roman
Catholic exposition of the Epistle.

According to Spicq Hebrews, together with the Apocalypse,
is farther removed from the modern Occidental mentality than
any other NT document. Its thoroughgoing affinity to the
language, imagery, theological concepts and mode of argument
of Philo leads Spicq to theorize that the author was a Philonist who, prior to his conversion to Christianity, was per-
sonally acquainted with the master himself. Thus although
the writer (probably Apollos) founded his doctrinal argument
on the Gospel tradition, direct literary and conceptual dependence upon Philo appears indisputable.[2]

---

1) *L'Épître aux Hébreux* Études Bibliques (2 vols.; Paris, 1952-53),
II, 179 ff.

2) Spicq's thesis that Hebrews was directly indebted to the writings
of Philo and that the Epistle therefore bears the unmistakable imprint
of Alexandrian religious philosophy is argued with great skill in the
chapter entitled: "Le philonisme de l'Épître aux Hébreux," I, 39-91.
However, R. Williamson has convincingly demonstrated via a thorough and
painstaking analysis of the data that linguistic similarities between
Hebrews and Philo are more superficial and coincidental than real. Furthermore, marked differences exist between the themes and ideas of the

Hebrews introduces Melchizedek as a prophetic type of the
priest of the New Covenant. Although Melchizedek's personal
worth was small, his typological significance was immense.
Curiously Melchizedek's bread and wine "offering" was omitted, even though it would have presented an exquisite pic-
ture of the heavenly service of the NT high priest. This
lacuna is accounted for in two ways: (i) unlike Paul who
attached great significance to the Eucharist,[1] the author
of Hebrews viewed Christ's priestly ministration in heaven
in relation to the cross and the heavenly sanctuary. (ii)
Furthermore, Hebrews so profoundly contrasts the iterated
sacrifice of the legal priests with the single self-sacri-
fice of Christ that mention of our Lord's offering on the
eve of his passion would have been most inappropriate.

Although typological exegesis predominates in Heb 7:1 ff.,
the author's *allegorical* exposition of the Genesis Melchizedek text in vs. 3 "is both the starting point and the center
of the argument of the chapter." The fact that according to
Semitic custom the life-data of significant figures were
punctiliously recorded suggests that the total absence of
such details in the case of one as prominent as Melchizedek
could only have been a matter of deliberate design. This
intentional silence vis-à-vis Melchizedek's human-temporal
relationships represents, in the words of Augustine, a great
"sacramentum" or "mysterium." Hebrews discovered a paradigm
for the deduction of esoteric spiritual truths in the Philonic *argumentum e silentio*. Did not the Alexandrian affirm
that absence of paternal and maternal ancestry was a persuasive demonstration not only of one's virtue and nobility
but also of one's divinity and immortality? Illumined by
the declaration of Psa 110:4, the writer of Hebrews was quick
to deduce from the silence of the OT affirmations which tran-
scended the historical sense of the ancient text.

If Melchizedek is introduced as having neither father
nor mother and if Scripture does not relate his death,

---

two writers and the manner in which each utilizes quotations from the
OT. Williamson concludes that "the influence of Philo on the writer of
Hebrews was minimal, perhaps even nonexistent." *Philo and the Epistle
to the Hebrews* (Leiden, 1970), 493.
 2) I Cor 11:23-25.

it is precisely because he is a type of the Son of God
without beginning and without end. Not having received
his priesthood from anyone and not having passed it on
to anyone else, he foreshadows the priesthood of Christ
at that point most fundamentally different from the Levitical priesthood.

Thus the two decisive results which emerge from the negative
features of the biblical portrait of Melchizedek are Christ's
absolute eternity and the uniqueness of his office.

Spicq's interpretation of ὅτι ζῇ (vs. 8) appears unique.
Noting that the subject of the verb is implicit rather than
explicit, Spicq affirms: "The intentional absence of any
mention of Melchizedek and Jesus Christ here has as its objective the association of type and antitype." To which is
added: "To be sure Jesus is dead like the Canaanite king,
but the priest is still living. Is not the immortal superior
to the mortal?"[1]

Member of the Society of Jesus, Albert Vanhoye (b. 1923),
has served for more than a decade as professor of NT at the
Pontifical Biblical Institute in Rome. Vanhoye has set forth
in his monograph on Hebrews[2] the most detailed and comprehensive analysis of the structure of the Epistle ever undertaken. Vanhoye maintains that the "mots-crochets" identified
by L. Vaganay in his analysis of the Epistle[3] provide the
key which deciphers the complex structure of the entire work.
Beginning with Vaganay's catch-words, which link one section
of the Epistle to another, Vanhoye added four additional literary criteria for the purpose of unfolding the plan of the
document: (i) the *announcement of the subject* to be considered; (ii) the *genre* of a given section (ie, doctrinal exposition or exhortation); (iii) *characteristic terms* which
impart to the development a distinct physiognomy; and (iv)

---

1) Spicq likens Hebrews' explication of the priesthood of Melchizedek
to Paul's appeal to the faith of Abraham (antedating the law) in his
Romans exposition of the doctrine of justification by faith. Both Hebrews
and Paul regarded the age of the patriarchs as an era of more spiritual
religion. Moses and the law represent a degeneration of the pristine
patriarchal faith, of which Christianity constitutes the rediscovery.

2) *La structure littéraire de l'Épître aux Hébreux*, Studia Neotestamentica I (Paris & Bruges, 1963), 125 ff.

3) "Le plan de l'Épître aux Hébreux," *Mémorial Lagrange* (Paris, 1940),
269-77.

118

inclusions which specify the limits of a given development.
Analyzing the Epistle by means of these five literary criteria, Vanhoye arrives at a broad outline which differs only
slightly from the plan of Vaganay. The uniqueness of Vanhoye's
work, however, resides in the highly detailed symmetry, balance and harmony which he discerns in this very intricate
and complex literary masterpiece.

Vanhoye treats Hebrews 7 as a single unit, assigning it
to the third and central division of his broad fivefold outline of the Epistle.[1] At the end of the second major division
(ch. 3:1-5:10), Vanhoye detects an *announcement of the subject* of the following division (ch. 5:11-10:39) in the words:
"being made perfect he became the source of eternal salvation to all who obey him, being designated by God high priest
after the order of Melchizedek" (ch. 5:9, 10). In addition,
he discovers that the three principal sections of the third
division follow the main outline of the *announcement of the
subject*. Hence Vanhoye entitles the three sections: III.A
(7:1-28), "Jesus high priest after the order of Melchizedek";
III.B (8:1-9:28), "Having attained perfection"; and III.C
(10:1-18), "Author of eternal salvation."

In the final verse of the preliminary exhortation (ch. 5:
11-6:20) to the third division, Vanhoye detects the *announcement of the subject* of ch. 7: "Jesus . . . high priest for
ever after the order of Melchizedek." The word "Melchizedek"
is identified as the "mot-crochet" which denotes the end of
the preliminary exhortation and the commencement of ch. 7.
Not only does "Melchizedek" function as the anterior catch-
word, but it is one of the *characteristic terms* of ch. 7 (vss.
1, 10, etc.), along with such words as "priest" (vss. 1, 3,
etc.), "law" (vss. 5, etc.) and "Levi" (vss. 5, 9, etc.).
Hebrews 7 lacks well-defined *inclusions*, although the final
sentence of the chapter (vs. 28), rich in antitheses, ful-
fills part of the function by recapitulating the teaching
of the chapter as a whole. Finally, it is noted that in common with the remainder of the third main division of the

---

1) a (Introduction) 1:1-4; I 1:5-2:18; II 3:1-5:10; III 5:11-10:39;
IV 11:1-12:13; V 12:14-13:19; z (Conclusion) 13:20-21.

Epistle, the *genre* of Hebrews 7 is "doctrinal exposition."

Having isolated ch. 7 as an independent unit of the third
and central division of the Epistle, Vanhoye applies his
literary criteria to a detailed analysis of the chapter itself. The criterion of *inclusions* shows that the chapter
divides into two smaller paragraphs, vss. 1-10 and vss. 11-
28, which by carefully conceived plan of the author are commentaries on Gen 14:17 ff. and Psa 110:4, respectively. The
first of the two subdivisions (the focus of the present study)
is isolated by observing that both the term "Melchizedek"
and the fact that Melchizedek "met" Abraham occur in vss.
1 and 10. Similarly, the second subdivision begins with the
word "perfection" and concludes with the participial form
"perfected," the latter word evoking recollections of the
announcement of the subject of the central division (ch. 5:
9). "Levi" (vs. 9) and "levitical" (vs. 11) function as catch-
words linking the two subdivisions of ch. 7. Furthermore,
these two paragraphs have been made to reflect on each other,
eg, the "they-he" (οἱ μὲν-ὁ δέ) contrast (cf vss. 5, 6 with
vss. 20, 21 and 23, 24) which highlights the superiority of
the new priestly order to the old.

By selective use of the same literary criteria Vanhoye
divides each of these subdivisions into still smaller units.
Limitations of space permit us only to illustrate the method.
The word "priest" (also the word "God"?) in vss. 1 and 3 is
identified as an *inclusion* which marks the *terminus a quo*
and *terminus ad quem* of the first of the two subsections of
vss. 1-10. Similarly, "Abraham" (vs. 4) and Levi's "ances-
tor" (vs. 10) (="Abraham," vs. 9) define the limits of the
second paragraph. The two subsections of vss. 1-10 are linked
internally by common reference to Melchizedek's blessing
(cf vs. 1 with vs. 6), the tithe (cf vs. 2 with vss. 4-6,
8-9), his mysterious origin (cf vs. 3 with vs. 6) and his
undying life (cf.vs. 3 with vs. 8). The two paragraphs neatly complement one another: the first depicts the enigmatic
person of Melchizedek, the latter unfolds his deeds and ac-
tions.

Explication of features of symmetry and balance, both in
respect of the principal divisions of the Epistle and also

120

in respect of the smallest paragraph, is executed with painstaking detail. By way of illustration, it is noted that the
incidents of the tithe, the blessing, and the meeting between
Melchizedek and Abraham in the two paragraphs of our text
(vss. 1-3 and vss. 4-10) are cited in reverse order, thus
providing a delicately balanced chiastic symmetry.

As for Melchizedek himself, Vanhoye observes that the ancient
figure is introduced with great solemnity.

> In a glorious period he sets before us Melchizedek in
> all his glorious titles. One feels he is striving to
> elevate his style to match the loftiness of his subject.
> . . . Between the explanation of the word "Salem" and
> the title "priest" the author inserts the interpretation
> of certain silences of the Bible. The omission of any
> indication of his age or ancestry somehow sets Melchiz-
> edek outside time. This kind of participation in eter-
> nity makes him a figure of the Son of God and permits
> one aspect of his priesthood to be brought to light: he
> remains a priest for ever.

Vanhoye's painstaking and detailed analysis has substantially enriched our understanding of the plan of the Epistle
and the interrelation of the parts within the whole.[1] Whether
the writer of Hebrews consciously designed such a complex
literary edifice, or whether Vanhoye has in places 'forced'
the text to fit a predetermined pattern remains a matter of
debate.

(c) Analysis of 11 Q Melchizedek

In 1956 thirteen fragments of a single column of a scroll
were discovered by Bedouin shepherds in what has become known
as Qumran Cave 11. When pieced together the manuscript por-
tion was found to be in an incomplete state with extensive

---

1) Undoubtedly Vanhoye's structural analysis will prove foundational
to future interpretation of the Epistle. Note the extensive use made of
Vanhoye's insights and terminology in the volume on Hebrews in the *Anchor Bible*: G.W. Buchanan, *To the Hebrews: Translation, Comment and
Conclusions* (Garden City, N.Y., 1972).

lacunae both within and between individual lines. Reconstruction of the fragmentary document was facilitated by the fact that approximately one-third of its contents consists of quotations from the OT. Since Melchizedek proves to be a leading figure in the document, the fragment has been named "11 Q Melchizedek." A. S. van der Woude published the *editio princeps* of the text of the manuscript in 1965 together with a German translation and explanatory annotations.[1]

The fragment when pieced together measures about 15 cm. by 17 cm., contains twenty-six lines of text and has been dated by van der Woude as a composition from the first half of the first Christian century.[2] It consists of a midrashic exposition of several OT texts (Lev 25:9, 10, 13; Deut 15: 2; Psa 7:8, 9; 82.1, 2; Isa 52:7; 61:1), the patent intention of which is to explicate the end-time salvation of the elect and the retribution which would be meted out upon the wicked. From the notions of redemption and restoration of possessions associated with the year of Jubilee (Lev 25:13), the writer contemplated as eschatological events the release from captivity and the return of the downtrodden children of light to the land of promise "at the end of days" (ie, the tenth Jubilee year).[3] The figure of Melchizedek emerges in the eschatological drama (1. 5) in the context of an allusion to Isa 61:1 announcing release and forgiveness for the elect presently bound by the powers of wickedness (1. 6). Lines 10 and 11 constitute the most significant part of the fragment. Psa 82:1, 2 is cited and, according to van der Woude, its meaning is transferred by the writer of the scroll to Melchizedek: "As it is written (10) concerning him in the hymns of David who says: 'The heavenly one (אלוהים; sing) *standeth* in the congre*gation of God*: among the heavenly ones (אלוהים; pl.) he judgeth,' and concerning him he says: '*Above* them (11) return thou on high; God shall judge the nations.'" Van der Woude concludes on several counts that the first

1) "Melchisedek als himmlische Erlösergestalt in den neugefundenen eschatologischen Midraschim aus Qumran-Höhle XI," *Oudtestamentische Studiën*, XIV (Leiden, 1965), 354-73.

2) *Ibid.*, 357.

3) Cf Dan 9:24-27.

אלוהיס designated Melchizedek himself: (i) the phrase "concerning him" (עליו; 1. 10) logically refers to Melchizedek who occupies a prominent position in the preceding line; (ii) God is consistently designated in the fragment not by אלוהים but by אל; (iii) in the context of the judgment (1. 13), Melchizedek is expressly differentiated from God; and (iv) the motif of the return to heaven by the אלוהים (ע[ליה למרום שוכה; 11. 10, 11 from Psa 7:7) would have been understood by contemporary Jews in terms of an angel. The plural אלוהים which follows agreeably refers to angels of lower rank than Melchizedek. Thus Melchizedek is depicted in the scroll as a paramount angelic figure who stands in the tribunal of God amidst a host of lesser angels. In lines 13 and 14, assisted by the supporting cast of just angels, Melchizedek executes eschatological judgment upon Belial and his band of perverse spirits.[1] In consequence of this retribution meted out upon the powers of darkness, the children of light are liberated for participation in the end-time salvation intimated in the prophetic word from Isa 61:1 (1. 6) and explicitly announced by the prophet in Isa 52:7 (11. 15 ff.). Attention ought also be drawn, in passing, to lines 24 and 25, where the text reads: "Thy heavenly one (אלוהיך) is king." Van der Woude argues that the sentence has reference to Melchizedek; only now his dominion is in view by virtue of his defeat of Belial and his company.[2] On the basis of the foregoing it is argued that this heavenly warrior-redeemer ought to be identified with Michael, the patron saint of Israel, who engages in an eschatological struggle with perverse spirits and who exercises in the heavenly temple a priestly ministry on behalf of the righteous.[3]

---

1) F. du Toit Laubscher proposes the following reading for the fragmentary thirteenth line: "And Melchizedek will exact the ve(nge)ance of the judg(m)ents of Go(d, and he will help all the Children of Light from the power of Be)lial and from the power of all (the spirits of) his (lot)." Accordingly, he thoroughly agrees with van der Woude that Melchizedek was a heavenly being. "God's Angel of Truth and Melchizedek: A note on 11 Q Melchizedek 13b," *Journal for the Study of Judaism*, 3 (1972), 46-51.

2) Cf reference to the "inheritance" (נחלה; 1. 5) and the "lot" (גורל; 1. 8) of Melchizedek.

3) Van der Woude maintains that the *priestly* side of Melchizedek is

In the final paragraph of his study, van der Woude proposed the following assessment of the relation of 11 Q Melchizedek to the priesthood Christology of Hebrews:

> Taking as a basis Psa 110:4 the author of Hebrews has
> clearly formulated his conception of the high priestly
> office of Jesus with the help of Jewish Melchizedek tra-
> dition reflected in 11 Q Melch. By this means he was
> able to demonstrate the incomparable superiority of the
> high priest according to the manner of Melchizedek over
> against the Levitical priests. The great statements about
> Melchizedek in Heb 7:2, 3, which had not been completely
> explicated by the author, were doubtless in his posses-
> sion and were rendered more fully intelligible by 11 Q
> Melch.

Not long after the appearance of the *editio princeps*, van
der Woude in conjunction with another Dutch scholar, M. de
Jonge, published an important article which reflects further painstaking study of this key Qumran document.[1] The
latter study offered, first, minor corrections to the text
and certain refinements of interpretation of 11 Q Melch. On
this basis the editors sought to demonstrate in considerable
detail the new light which allegedly is cast upon Heb 7:1 ff.
by this first century scroll from Cave 11. A notable advance
in the second study is the reluctance of de Jonge and van
der Woude to assert the unqualified identification of Melchizedek with the arch-angel Michael.[2] This note of caution
is prompted by the recognition that "11 Q Melch. gives no
certain reference to a (high-) priesthood of Melchizedek.
He is so much 'God's warrior' that his priestly activities
remain completely in the shadow."

To what extent, then, is the message of our text clarified by the evidence of 11 Q Melch? De Jonge and van der
Woude affirm at the outset that Melchizedek's name ("king
of righteousness") and title ("king of peace") constitute
"the great eschatological gifts of God." The statement of
Heb 7:3 could not have been formulated solely on the basis

---

amply illustrated by the Jewish (Gen 14:18 ff.; Psa 110:4) and Christian
Scriptures (Heb 7:1).

1) "11 Q Melchizedek and the New Testament," *NTS*, 12 (1965-66), 301-
26.

2) Van der Woude's earlier cited appeal to the priestly attributes
of the *biblical* Melchizedek lent little support to his thesis that the
angel warrior of 11 Q Melch. is to be identified with the archangel
Michael.

of data from Gen 14:17 ff., but must be attributed to oral
or written tradition. How are the key epithets ἀπάτωρ, ἀμήτωρ,
κτλ to be understood? Could the writer have modelled a human,
historical Melchizedek after the pattern of the Son of God
via an *argumentum e silentio*? The Dutch scholars discount
this possibility as very remote and add:

> It seems much easier to assume that the author really
> meant what he wrote. On the evidence of 11 Q Melch. the
> most plausible inference is that he regarded Melchizedek
> as an (arch)angel, who appeared to Abraham long ago.

The heavenly warrior-redeemer thus occupied a highly exalted
status in the eschatological schema of first century Jewish
sectarian expectation. Nevertheless, lest his readers be
tempted to elevate Melchizedek above Christ himself, the
writer of Hebrews consciously subordinated his dignity to
that of the eternal Son by means of the qualifying clause
ἀφωμοιωμένος δὲ τῷ υἱῷ τοῦ θεοῦ. Although the priestly dignity of the paramount ministrant is vastly superior to the
earthbound priesthood of Levi, Melchizedek is but a figure
of the One whose eminence over all angelic beings earlier
had been established in the Epistle (chs. 1, 2). Thus not
as a human personality who emerges and mysteriously vanishes
from view, but precisely as a heavenly (arch)angel is Melchizedek represented in Hebrews 7 as a priest who remains
for ever.

In an appendix to the article under consideration, the
authors set out to demonstrate that the Melchizedek consciousness of the writer of Hebrews was in agreement with the views
of certain of the orthodox fathers of the church. The Alexandrian theologians Origen and his pupil Didymas judged that
Melchizedek was an angel, whereas Cyril of Alexandria wrote
that other authorities regarded Melchizedek as a heavenly
δύναμις (=ἄγγελος?). In Gnostic circles, however, (especially
the heretical Melchizedekians), a wide range of speculation
flourished which portrayed Melchizedek as a heavenly power
superior to Christ himself. According to one Theodotos, Melchizedek was the highest of divine powers, his descent to
earth prior to Christ demonstrating his precedence to the
latter. De Jonge and van der Woude maintain that although
regarded by Hebrews as an heavenly (arch)angel, Melchizedek's

subservience to Christ was carefully preserved by the writer
in the argument of ch. 7:3.

The American Jesuit scholar, J. A. Fitzmyer, in a study
which followed upon van der Woude's *editio princeps*, gave
further consideration to the Qumran fragment.[1] The format
of his study--reconstructed Hebrew text, translation and interpretive annotations--is similar to that of the Dutch scholars. Fitzmyer agrees in the main with the judgment of de
Jonge and van der Woude as to the interpretation of the document, but his estimate of the relationship of 11 Q Melch. to
Hebrews differs considerably from that of his Dutch colleagues.

Fitzmyer observes that Melchizedek's representation in
the Qumran text as a heavenly figure elevated above the angelic host in the context of a day of atonement and retribution, sheds additional light on the relationship enunciated by Hebrews between Melchizedek and the high priest of
the New Covenant. In particular, if Melchizedek were regarded
as the "herald" of the Isaian text, one could detect signs
of a conflation of OT titles in respect of the eschatological figure not unlike the titles ascribed to Christ in the
NT. Thus 11 Q Melch.'s "exaltation of Melchizedek and its
view of him as a heavenly redemption-figure make it understandable how the author of the Epistle to the Hebrews could
argue for the superiority of Christ the high priest over the
levitical priesthood by appeal to such a figure." Beyond
elucidation of the Melchizedek-Christ correspondence, Fitzmyer argues that it is quite improbable that the author of
Hebrews derived his conception of Melchizedek from the consciousness of Qumran. The tradition about Melchizedek reflected in Heb 7:1 ff. must be differentiated from that of
11 Q Melch. in precisely the respect that the Qumran document expounds the heavenly warrior-redeemer with virtually
no regard for the Genesis and Psalm texts which were foundational to the argument of Hebrews 7. Thus the Melchizedek
motifs reflected in 11 Q Melch. and Hebrews 7 appear to be
derived from parallel rather than interdependent first cen-

---

1) "Further Light on Melchizedek from Qumran Cave 11," *JBL*, 86 (1967),
25-41.

tury traditions.

Not long after the publication of van der Woude's *editio princeps*, Yigael Yadin, professor of archaeology at the Hebrew University of Jerusalem wrote a short article[1] in which he proposed several alternative readings to van der Woude's reconstructed Hebrew text[2] and offered his own estimate of the relevance of 11 Q Melch. for an understanding of the role of Melchizedek in Hebrews. According to Yadin, the heavenly station of the angelic Melchizedek in the Qumran fragment cannot be refuted. The remarkable feature of 11 Q Melch., however, is the convincing evidence which it provides in respect of a question which remained unanswered in his previous study on the relationship of Hebrews to the Dead Sea Scrolls:[3] "How and why did the author (ie, of Hebrews) come to use Melchizedek as his main theme?" With the recovery of 11 Q Melch. the mystery has been immeasurably clarified.

> It seems that now we have the answer; since Melchizedek was considered to have had such a heavenly position, as well as an active role as an eschatological saviour, in the Qumranite theology, the writer chose him deliberately, in order to convey more intimately and decisively his perception of Jesus' unique position.

J. Carmignac in his analysis of 11 Q Melch.[4] arrives at a conclusion which is fundamentally opposed to that of the

---

1) "A Note on Melchizedek and Qumran," *IEJ*, 15 (1965), 152-54.

2) The most important variant (which is not immediately related to the present study) is found in 1. 18 of the fragment which comprises part of the *pesher* of Isa 52:17. The main issue concerns the identity of the מבשר of the Isaian citation. Van der Woude rendered the text fragment immediately following as, הו[א]ה המ[ש]יח הוא[ה], which he translates: "das ist der Messias." God's Messiah announces the advent of the promised eschatological salvation. Fitzmyer, accepting the preceding Hebrew reading of 1. 18, elects to restore at the end of the line the word דניאל. Thereby he argues that the "herald" of Isa 52:7 is the "Anointed One," in particular, the משיח נגיד of Dan 9:25. However, Yadin concludes that the reading proposed by van der Woude is falsely contrived. Accordingly, Yadin suggests the alternative reading, הואה מ[שוח הרו]ח, which favors the view that the "herald" is the prophet anointed by the Spirit who in Isa 61:1 bears good tidings to the downtrodden (cf 1. 6). De Jonge and van der Woude were quick to adopt the reading proposed by the Hebrew scholar in their later article. Thus they affirmed that משיח הרוח is likely "the Prophet" of sectarian expectation who appears along with "the Messias of Aaron and Israel" in I QS 9:11.

3) "The Dead Sea Scrolls and the Epistle to the Hebrews," *Scripta Hierosolymitana*, 4 (1958), 36-55.

4) "Le document de Qumran sur Melkisedeq," *RQ*, VII (1970), 343-78.

preceding scholars. On no account should the Melchizedek of
the scroll be identified as an angel. The French scholar
maintains that the principal theme of the fragmentary scroll
is not Melchizedek but the execution of divine judgment upon
the powers of Belial and the consequent liberation of the
righteous. In particular, the introductory formulas to the
all important citations from Psalm 82 and Psalm 7, preserved
in lines 10 and 11, relate to the theme of the judgment of
God (prominent in the immediate context) rather than to Melchizedek himself. Carmignac's translation of lines 10 and
11 reflects this interpretation.[1]

According to Carmignac, the two appearances of אלוהים
is Psa 82:1 relate not to Melchizedek the paramount angel
and the company of lesser angels, respectively, but to God
himself and the saints of the congregation.

Having set aside the interpretation that Melchizedek was
viewed as an angel, and likewise having discounted the view
that the scroll has reference to the figure of the patriarchal history, Carmignac suggests that 11 Q Melch. depicts
a terrestrial figure associated with the Qumran community.
The identity and function of this figure becomes more evident if we regard him as the "symbolic" or "etymological"
Melchizedek. From the point of view of the former appelative,
the figure in the scroll is symbolically descriptive of a
warrior-chief who would arise and emulate in his person and
mission the biblical Melchizedek. The etymological Melchizedek signifies the figure who would preserve the etymological
sense of מלכי-צדק and who would be acclaimed, by executing
the judgment of God, as "Roi parfaitement juste." Carmignac
suggests that the reference in l. 18 to one "consacré de
l'esprit" reinforces the conviction that the Melchizedek
of the scroll would be none other than the Messiah of Israel[2]
who would arise from the sectarian community to annihilate
the impious and liberate the children of light.

---

1) "Comme il est écrit à son sujet dans les cantiques de David, qui
dit: 'Dieu [se ti]ent dans l'as[semblée des saints,] au milieu des
(êtres) divins il jugera.' Et à son sujet, de [nouveau, a été ré]alisé:
'Retourne dans les hauteurs. Dieu jugera les peuples.'"

2) 1 QS 9:11; I QSa 2:14, 20; CDC 12:23; 14:19 etc.

According to this interpretation of 11 Q Melch., the author of Hebrews contemplated Melchizedek not as an arch-
angel who appeared to Abraham, but as an historical figure
who served as a prefigurative model of the Christ. By means
of an allegorical exegesis, by which he drew Melchizedek and
Christ into a most intimate relation (vss. 3, 15), the writer
of the Epistle regarded Melchizedek as an historical figure
whose character and function would be reproduced by the Messiah to come. Thus Carmignac concludes:

> Since the Melchizedek of Qumran is to him an historical
> person who will reproduce the features of the biblical
> Melchizedek (or who will verify the significance of his
> name, "king of Justice"), the mode of argumentation of
> the Epistle to the Hebrews is exactly the same as that
> which we have established in our document.

Thus whereas a few Qumran scholars are convinced that 11
Q Melch. depicts a terrestrial figure, the majority interpret Heb 7:3 in the light of the scroll's apparent representation of Melchizedek as a heavenly angel warrior who executes eschatological judgment upon the powers of darkness.

V. CONCLUSION

That Melchizedek's shadowy encounter with Abraham in Gen 14:18 ff. and subsequent mention in the oracle of Psalm 110 has stimulated widespread speculation in Jewish and Christian circles as to the identity of this furtive figure is evident from the history. In pre-Christian Samaritan tradition[1] the meeting between Melchizedek and Abraham recorded in the Genesis text is alleged to have occured on Gerizim, the holy mountain of the sect. Not only is Salem, the seat of Melchizedek's rule, identified with Shechem, but the mountain itself (ὄρος ὑψίστου) is named after Melchizedek, the "priest of God most high." Furthermore, Melchizedek figured prominently in the establishment of the sanctuary and the worship of the Samaritans, apparently as their first priest. Later Samaritan tradition of a highly syncretistic character identified Melchizedek as a purely mythological figure whose parents were Heracles and Ashtoreth. A recently recovered fragment of a Qumran scroll entitled "11 Q Melchizedek," which van der Woude identifies as a composition from the first half of the first Christian century indicates that Melchizedek may have been regarded by the Qumran community as an eschatological angel-warrior who preserves the faithful and executes judgment on the perverse angels.[2] In the philosophical religion of Philo of Alexandria Melchizedek, "the righteous king" and the "king of peace," is allegorically depicted as a manifestation of the high priestly Logos

---

1) The earliest Samaritan traditions concerning Melchizedek were handed down by Alexander Polyhistor (b. 105 BC) via Eusebius. For a summary of the evidence see Gerd Theissen, *Untersuchungen zum Hebräerbrief*, Studien zum Neuen Testament 2 (Gütersloh, 1969), 17 ff., 130 ff. The Samaritan account of Melchizedek must be considered in the light of the fact that Samaritan tradition transferred individual events of the patriarchal history from their original setting to Mt. Gerizim, the revered site of the sect's sanctuary. Cf *EJ*, VII, 436, 437.

2) The author of Hebrews may have been aware of the existence of such speculation which regarded Melchizedek as an angel. Yet his extraordinary emphasis upon the humanity of Jesus (who subsequently was exalted to heavenly priesthood) suggests that the writer may have consciously striven to *refute* all such mystical speculation.

who intoxicates the soul with esoteric virtues. In post-bib-
lical thought the notion of an angelic Messianic figure also
known to Qumran was developed even further. Late Jewish apocalyptic literature variously interpreted Melchizedek as a
heavenly angel exercising priestly functions, as the arch-
angel Michael himself, or as a high priest of the Messianic
age who emerges alongside Elijah *redivivus*. Mythical material
preserved in an appendix to the Slavonic Book of Enoch ("The
Priesthood of Methuselah, Noah and Melchizedek") depicts the
miraculous conception of Melchizedek and his birth from the
corpse of Sopanima the wife of Nir, brother of Noah. Likely
a Christian legend with Gnostic coloring, the myth continues
with the prophecy that Melchizedek will reign as a priest
and king in the middle of the earth as a prototype of the
Messiah.[1] Finally, the Christian "Book of Adam in the East,"
a mythical Christian-Gnostic reworking of a Jewish Adam legend, regards Melchizedek as an incarnation of the Primal Man
and bearer of an end-time high priesthood. Many of the preceding examples of Melchizedek speculation are clearly mythological representations which postdate the composition of
Hebrews.[2] Gerd Theissen concludes that the only extra-biblical pre-Christian antecedents to the Melchizedek motif
which warrant serious consideration are those preserved in
the traditions of the Samaritans and in the literature of
Philo and the Qumran community.[3] However, previous consideration of these three possible sources suggests that direct
dependence of Hebrews upon Samaritan, Philonic or Qumranite
Melchizedek speculation is highly improbable.

A more responsible alternative to the preceding specula-

---

1) See G.N. Bonwetsch, *Die Bücher der Geheimnisse Henochs, TU* 44/2
(Leipzig, 1922) 116-21. Also R.H. Charles, *The Book of the Secrets of
Enoch* (Oxford, 1896), 85-93. Charles identifies the legend as the work
of a first century Christian heretic, although A.J.B. Higgins argues
more convincingly for a later date of composition. "The Priestly Messiah," *NTS* 13 (1966/67), 212. A post-Christian dating of the material
is to be preferred as the legend appears to be a patent mythological
development of the Synoptic accounts of the birth of John the Baptist
and Jesus.
2) As a working hypothesis we date Hebrews as a composition origi-
nating from the seventh decade of the first Christian century.
3) *Untersuchungen*, 130.

tion would be to suggest that Hebrews' development of the
Melchizedek motif was drawn directly from the Messianic prophecy of Psa 110:4. Since the full significance of this text
was not immediately clear, the writer turned to Gen 14:18
ff., the only other citation of Melchizedek in Scripture, to
discover what the Psalmist had intended by the words "priest
for ever after the order of Melchizedek."[1] Thus the writer
in Heb 7:1 ff. explicates the Psalm text by a typological
exposition of the antecedent Pentateuchal narrative for the
purpose of demonstrating the superiority of Christ, the antitypical Melchizedek, to the priests of Aaron. Hebrews fully
regards Melchizedek as an historical figure who united kingship with the worship and service of the God of Abraham in
the midst of a pagan culture. Josephus appears close to the
matter when he affirms that Melchizedek was a genuine personality of antiquity, "a potent man among the Canaanites"
who on the basis of uprightness of character was a priest
of the true God.[2]

Via the explanatory particle γάρ (vs. 1), the author proceeds to explicate in detail the meaning and implications
of the declaration of the Psalmist that Christ is a "high
priest for ever after the order of Melchizedek" (ch. 6:20).
In order to unfold the profound significance of this radically new priestly order, the writer offers a terse recitation
and interpretation of selected features of the Genesis narrative. Clearly the author holds the OT in high esteem, regarding the ancient Scriptures as the embodiment of the
counsels of God. The principal thesis of the lengthy opening
sentence (vss. 1-3) is the main clause: Οὗτος γὰρ ὁ Μελχισέδεκ . . . μένει ἱερεὺς εἰς τὸ διηνεκές. Further arguments
adduced both from the declarations and the silences of the
Genesis narrative amplify the major theme of the *perpetuity*
of the ancient non-Levitical priestly ministrant. The au-

---

1) Cf G.B. Caird, "The Exegetical Method of the Epistle to the Hebrews," *CJT*, 5 (1959), 48. Thus the messianic typology of Hebrews bears
a close resemblance to the *rāz-pesher* schema of Qumran exegesis. See
F.F. Bruce, *Biblical Exegesis in the Qumran Texts* (London, 1960), 7 ff.,
75 ff.
2) *Ant*. I. 10. 2; *Wars* VI. 10. 1.

thor's interpretation of Gen 14:18 ff. displays similarities
to the hermeneutics of Alexandrian Judaism, particularly in
the significance which it attaches to the silence of the
biblical account. Hebrews recounts with interest that Melchizedek, unlike the Hebrew kings, united in his person the
dual honors of royalty and priesthood. One falsely concludes
from the designation ἱερεὺς τοῦ θεοῦ τοῦ ὑψίστου (vs. 1) that
Melchizedek was a polytheist who officiated before the highest of a host of lesser deities. Philo correctly comprehends
the sense of the title; the Logos, of whom Melchizedek is
a shadow, "is priest of the Most High, not that there is any
other not Most High--for God being one 'is in heaven above
and on earth beneath, and there is none beside Him! (Deut
4:39)."[1]

The writer's typical interpretation of Melchizedek's proper name and title (vs. 2) reflects the significance which
Oriental cultures and the Jews, in particular, attached to
personal names. Philo[2] and Josephus[3] translate the Hebrew
name "Melchizedek" as βασιλεὺς δίκαιος, although Hebrews'
translation of βασιλεὺς δικαιοσύνης is equally justifiable
on etymological grounds and is even more descriptive of the
Messianic antitype who both rules with justice and dispenses
righteousness to the subjects of his realm.[4] Similarly, the
interpretation of Melchizedek's royal title is a further
characterization of the Messianic priest of the new order.[5]
The author shows little interest in the precise location of
the seat of Melchizedek's reign; rather he is content to
deduce from the etymological derivation of his name and title
two principal features of the end-time priest-king.[6]

Vs. 3 clearly constitutes the great exegetical conundrum
of the chapter, a correct understanding of which is essential for a proper appreciation both of the uniqueness of
Melchizedek and the priest after his order. The great diver-

---

1) *Leg. alleg.* III. 82.
2) *Leg. alleg.* III. 79.
3) *Ant.* I. 10. 180; *Wars* VI. 10.
4) Isa 32:1; Jer 23:5, 6; 33:15 ff.; Mal 4:2; I Cor 1:30; Heb 1:8, 9.
5) I Chron 22:9; Zech 9:10; Eph 2:14 ff.
6) Psa 72:1, 7; Isa 9:6 ff.; 32:17; Rom 14:17; Test. Jud 24:1.

sity of opinion which surrounds the interpretation of this
key text is an indication of its obscurity and difficulty.
We may well perceive in the verse characteristics of a little hymn in which is preserved a tradition of the primitive
church.[1] The history has demonstrated that a literal acceptance of the epithets of vs. 3 has spawned a flood of fanciful speculation about a supra-human priestly figure. By re-
cognizing that not only what Scripture expressly declares
in respect of Melchizedek but furthermore what it *does not
declare* is of immense significance to the author, may we
eliminate much of the conjecture which has been advanced.
The rabbis commonly regarded as non-existent what was not
expressly recorded in their sacred documents. Thus since the
father of a Gentile was not enumerated in the Jewish genealogies, the latter was characterized by the Jews as ἀπάτωρ.[2]
The same *argumentum e silentio*, whereby the silence of Scripture was frought with significance, was a commonplace interpretive device in the hermeneutical schema of Alexandrian
Judaism. In more than one place Philo characterizes Sarah
as ἀμήτωρ on the ground that no mention is made of her mother in Scripture.[3] Thus we conclude that Hebrews depicts Melchizedek as ἀπάτωρ, ἀμήτωρ, ἀγενεαλόγητος since no mention
is made in the Genesis record of his mother, father and genealogy. Not the historical Melchizedek as such, but the
typical or prophetic figure who appears on the pages of Scripture is devoid of parentage and descent. The final term of
the triad (without pedigree, "of unrecorded descent"[4]), which
amplifies the meaning of the first two terms, argues convincingly for the preferred interpretation. Absence of recorded parentage and genealogy in the case of one so eminent

---

1) G. Wuttke (1927), G. Schille (1955) and H. Zimmermann (1964) regard vss. 1-3 in their entirety as hymnodic, whereas O. Michel (1966)
judges that vs. 3 alone is poetic material. G. Theisson (1969) much more
ambitiously suggests that ch. 7 as a whole represents an elaboration of
a larger hymn of six stanzas. On the other hand, F. Schröger (1968) argues that it cannot be conclusively proven that the author incorporated
any hymnodic traditions in vss. 1-3.
2) Bereshith R. XVIII. 18. 2.
3) *De ebr.* 61; *Quis rer.* 62.
4) *LSJ*, I, 8. The final term of the triad is not to be rendered "without descent," which would require the Greek ἀγένητος.

as Melchizedek was contrary to the usual practice of the
chroniclers of Jewish history and thus evoked considerable
speculation as to his identity. The paramount reason why
Melchizedek was described in such terms was to emphasize his
complete disassociation from the legal priestly regime. The
eminent priest-king who blessed the patriarch and who col-
lected tithes from the progenitor of Aaron, had no link with
the disenfranchised tribe of Levi. In contrast to the legal
priests for whom paternal descent from Aaron[1] and maternal
descent from a pure Israelite[2] was mandatory (and who were
disqualified from service if incapable of proving priestly
descent[3]), this priest-king exercised a royal priestly service solely on the basis of his innate worth. So understood,
"this man who has not their genealogy" (vs. 6), admirably
adumbrates the Messianic priest who was descended from the
non-sacerdotal tribe of Judah (vss. 13, 14). The traditional
view that Melchizedek foreshadowed Christ insofar as the latter was ἀπάτωρ and ἀμήτωρ with respect to his humanity and
divinity, respectively, probably was not intended by the
writer.

The second line of the little hymn, μήτε ἀρχὴν ἡμερῶυ μήτε
ζωῆς τέλος ἔχων likewise is to be interpreted on the basis
of the silence of the Genesis narrative, no mention being
made in Scripture of Melchizedek's birth and death. By various means exegetes have interpreted this text in terms of
the commencement and termination of priestly life, either
with reference to the priests proper or the Levites, but not
without forced results. As Delitzsch rightly observed, the
text cannot be restricted to imply mere absence of data concerning Melchizedek's accession or succession to priestly
office: "The words are intended to express much more than
this very limited sense."[4] Moreover, such an interpretation
would introduce in vs. 3 a needless tautology. Thus via an
argument from silence the author negates the commencement
and termination of Melchizedek's natural life, thereby in-

---

1) Exod 28:1; Numb 3:10; 18:1.
2) Lev 21:7; 13 ff.; Ezek 44:22.
3) Ezra 2:62; Neh 7:63 ff.
4) *Hebräer*, 271.

sisting on the absolute eternity of his personal, albeit
typical, existence. Melchizedek is portrayed as one who suddenly emerged from the distant reaches of eternity and who
later vanished into its depths just as mysteriously. It is
precisely the notion of eternity, foreshadowed in Melchizedek
and realized in Christ, which repeatedly emerges as the leading refrain and the unifying feature of the text and of Hebrews as a whole. Hereby the mystery surrounding the previous epithets is clarified; the incarnate Son of God--eter-
nal *a parte ante* and *a parte post*--had no need of human
priestly ancestry to legitimize his unique and never-ending
priesthood.

The particle δέ effects the transition from the negative
predicates to the positive assertion ἀφωμοιωμένος δὲ τῷ υἱῷ
τοῦ θεοῦ, which provides a rational basis for the transfer
of statements about the ancient *Abbild* to the Messianic
Urbild. The perfect participial form of the NT *hapax legomenon*
ἀφομοιοῦν denotes that from the perspective of the biblical
narrative Melchizedek has been "made like" or "made to resemble" the Son of God.[1] The clause suggests that on the
basis of his characterization in the Genesis record, Melchizedek is invested with a symbolic resemblance to the antitypical priest of the New Covenant. The question has been
extensively debated as to those points of correspondence
between Melchizedek and Christ which the author sought to
convey by this expression, which provides justification for
the statement that Melchizedek μένει ἱερεύς εἰς τὸ διηνεκές.
Clearly the principal point of correspondence resides in
those predicates immediately preceding ἀφωμοιωμένος which
enunciate the eternity of their respective persons; yet the
author's conception of Melchizedek as a model of the high
priest of the New Covenant includes at least two other sub-
sidiary notions. Thus we suggest that the Melchizedek of the
Genesis narrative serves as a fitting type of Christ in the
following respects: (i) Melchizedek was a harbinger of the
"king of righteousness" and "king of peace" who would unite
in his person priestly prerogatives with royalty; (ii) he

---

1) *AG*, 126; cf RSV; J. Moffatt, *Hebrews*, 93.

foreshadowed Christ insofar as the legitimacy of his priesthood was founded not upon physical descent from a priestly
regime but solely on the basis of innate personal worth and
divine appointment; and supremely (iii) Melchizedek was an
earthly figure of the eternal Son of God who in reality possesses neither beginning nor end of personal existence.

The logical conclusion of the matter is that the one who
so fittingly adumbrates the Son of God, μένει ἱερεὺς εἰς τὸ
διηνεκές. The history of this text has shown that many interpreters have been reluctant to apply these words to Melchizedek. Thus not a few have linked them to Christ either
explicitly by inserting a relative before the verb, or im-
plicitly by postulating absorption of the type into the antitype. Εἰς τὸ διηνεκές is a refinement of the phrase εἰς τὸν
αἰῶνα and indicates precisely how the writer understood the
ascription of eternity in the Psalm text. Unique to the NT
and the LXX εἰς τὸ διηνεκές gives up its meaning when it is
observed that in Gen 14:18 ff. Melchizedek's priestly service was neither taken up from a predecessor nor was it handed
on to a successor. The silence of the record invests Melchizedek with an intransmissible and hence continuous priesthood
which symbolically portrays the unbounded perpetuity of the
priesthood of Christ.

Vs. 8 underscores the teaching of vs. 3 and highlights
a principal feature of Melchizedek's superiority to the priests
of Levi. Whereas those appointed to priestly service by the
law succumbed to death and hence gave way to a series of
successors, Scripture announces of Melchizedek only the fact
of his living. This declaration of continuance in life is
equivalent to the affirmation deduced from the Genesis record
that beginning of days and end of life are wanting. The
priest who stands forth in Scripture in the power of life
administers a priesthood which is absolute and inviolable.
How fitting, in anticipation of Christ, that we read of the
one who blessed and tithed the patriarch and whose life is
said to be impervious to death, "See how great he is!" (vs.
4).

SELECTED BIBLIOGRAPHY

ALEXANDER, J. P.: *A Priest Forever: A Study of the Epistle Entitled "To The Hebrews."* London, 1937.

ALFORD, H.: "ΠΡΟΣ ΕΒΡΑΙΟΥΣ" in *The Greek Testament*. New Edition. London and New York, 1897-1903. Vol. IV, pp. 1-273.

AUBERLEN, K. A.: "Melchisedek's ewiges Leben und Priesterthum: Hebr. 7." *ThSK* 30 (1857), 453-504.

BAIER, J. W.: *Compendium theologiae positivae*. Ed. by E. Preuss. Berolinum, 1864.

BARCLAY, W.: *The Letter to the Hebrews*. The Daily Study Bible. Philadelphia, 1957.

BARDY, G.: "Melchisédech dans la tradition patristique." *RB* 35 (1926), 496-509; 36 (1927), 25-45.

BAUER, W.: *Grieschisch-Deutsches Wörterbuch zu den Schriften des NT*. 4th. ed. Berlin, 1949-52.

BENGEL, J. A.: "In epistolam ad Hebraeos" in *Gnomon Novi Testamenti*. 3rd. ed. Tubinga, 1773. Pp. 885-936. ET: "On the Epistle to the Hebrews" in *Gnomon of the New Testament*. Edinburgh, 1857-58. Vol. IV, pp. 333-502.

BEZA, T.: *Jesu Christi Domini Nostri Novum Testamentum*. 5th. ed. Geneva, 1598. Vol. II, pp. 386-440.

BIESENTHAL, J. H. R.: *Das Trostschreiben des Apostels Paulus an die Hebräer*. Leipzig, 1878.

BISPING, A.: *Erklärung des Briefes an die Hebräer*. Münster, 1854.

BLEEK, F.: *Der Brief an die Hebräer*. 3 vols. Berlin, 1828-40.

————.: *Einleitung in das Neue Testament*. 2 vols. Berlin, 1860-62.

BÖHME, C. F.: *Epistola ad Hebraeos latine vertit atque commentario instruxit perpetuo*. Lipsia, 1825.

BONSIRVEN, J.: *Saint Paul: Épître aux Hébreux*. Verbum Salutis 12. Paris, 1943.

BRAMBERG, C.: "Melchisedech." *Erbe und Auftrag* 40 (1964), 5-21.

BRAUN, J.: *Commentarius in epistolam ad Hebraeos*. Amstelodamum, 1705.

BRUCE, A. B.: *The Epistle to the Hebrews: The First Apology for Christianity*. Edinburgh, 1899.

BRUCE, F. F.: *The Epistle to the Hebrews*. NIC. London and Edinburgh, 1965.

————.: *Biblical Exegesis in the Qumran Texts*. London, 1960.

138

BUCHANAN, G. W.: *To The Hebrews: Translation, Comment and Conclusions*. The Anchor Bible. Garden City, N.Y., 1972.

BÜCHSEL, F.: *Die Christologie des Hebräerbriefes*. Beiträge zur Förderung christlicher Theologie XXVII.2. Gütersloh, 1922.

BURCH, V.: *The Epistle to the Hebrews: Its Sources and Message*. London, 1936.

CALMET, A.: "Commentaire littéral sur l'Épître aux Hébreux" in *Commentaire littéral sur les Épîtres de saint Paul*. Paris, 1716. Vol. II, pp. 552-789.

CALOV, A.: "Annotata in epistolam ad Ebraeos" in *Biblia Novi Testamenti illustrata*. Francofurtum, 1676. Vol. III, pp. 1094-1388.

CALVIN, J.: "Commentarius in epistolam ad Hebraeos" in *CR*. Vol. LXXXIII, col. 9-198. ET: *Commentaries on the Epistle of Paul the Apostle to the Hebrews*. Edinburgh, 1853.

_____: *Institutio christianae religionis*. Vol. XXX of *CR*. ET: *Institutes of the Christian Religion*. 3 vols. Edinburgh, 1845-46.

_____: "Trois sermons sur l'histoire de Melchisédec" in *CR*. Vol. LI, col. 641-82.

CAMERON, J.: "Ad quaestiones in epistolam ad Hebraeos" in *Praelectiones in selectoria quaedam NT loca*. Salmurum, 1626-28. Vol. III, pp. 129-267.

_____: *Myrothecium evangelicum, in quo aliquot loca Novi Testamenti explicantur*. Geneva, 1632.

CAPPEL, J.: "Observationes in epistolam ad Hebraeos" in *Observationes in Novum Testamentum*. Ed. by L. Cappel. Amstelodamum, 1657, pp. 102-300.

CARMIGNAC, J.: "Le document de Qumran sur Melchisédeq." *RQ* 7 (1970), 343-78.

CARPZOV, J. B.: *Sacrae exercitationes in S. Paulli epistolam ad Hebraeos ex Philone Alexandrino*. Helmstadium, 1750.

CHEYNE, T. K.: "Melchizedek." *Encyclopedia Biblica*. London, 1899-1903. Vol. III, pp. 3014 ff.

COCCEIUS, J.: *Epistola ad Hebraeos: explicatio et veritatis ejus demonstratio*. Lugdunum Batavorum, 1659.

CRAMER, J. A.: *Erklärung des Briefes Pauli an die Hebräer*. 2 vols. Kopenhagen & Leipzig, 1757.

CULLMANN, O.: *Die Christologie des Neuen Testaments*. 2nd. ed. Tübingen, 1958. ET: *The Christology of the New Testament*. 2nd. ed. London, 1963.

DAVIDSON, A. B.: *The Epistle to the Hebrews*. Handbooks for Bible Classes. Edinburgh, 1882.

DELITZSCH, F.: *Commentar zum Briefe an die Hebräer*. Leipzig, 1857. ET: *Commentary on the Epistle to the Hebrews*. 2 vols. Edinburgh, 1868-70.

DIBELIUS, M.: "Der himmlische Kultus nach dem Hebräerbrief." *Theologische Blätter* 21 (1942), 1-11.

DODS, M.: "The Epistle to the Hebrews" in *EGT*. London, 1897-1910. Vol. IV, pp. 221-381.

DORSCHEUS, J.: *In epistolam divi Pauli ad Ebraeos commentarius*. Francofurtum & Lipsia, 1717.

EBRARD, J. H. A.: *Der Brief an die Hebräer*. Olshausen's Biblischer Commentar des Neuen Testaments. V.2. Königsberg, 1850.

EDWARDS, T. C.: *The Epistle to the Hebrews*. Expositor's Bible. 2nd. ed. London, 1888.

ERASMUS, D.: "Epistola Pauli apostoli ad Hebraeos" in *Desiderii Erasmi opera omnia*. Lugdunum Batavorum, 1703-7. Vol. VI, col. 983-1024.

_____: "In epistolam ad Hebraeos paraphrasis" in *opera omnia*. Vol. VII, col. 1165-98.

ESTIUS, W.: *In omnes Pauli epistolas item in catholicas commentarii*. Moguntia, 1841-45. Vol. VI, pp. 176 ff.

EWALD, G. H.: *Das Sendschreiben an die Hebräer und Jakobos' Rundschreiben übersetzt und erklärt*. Göttingen, 1870.

_____: *Die Lehre der Bibel von Gott, oder Theologie des alten und neuen Bundes*. 4 vols. Leipzig, 1871-76.

FARRAR, F. W.: *The Epistle of Paul the Apostle to the Hebrews*. CGTSC. Cambridge, 1894.

FITZMYER, J. A.: "Further Light on Melchizedek from Qumran Cave 11." *JBL* 86 (1967), 25-41.

_____: "'Now This Melchizedek . . .' (Heb. 7:1)." *CBQ* 25 (1963), 305-21.

FRIEDLÄNDER, M.: "La secte de Melchisédec et l'Épître aux Hébreux." *Revue des études juives* 5 (1882), 1-26; 6 (1883), 187-99.

GERHARD, J.: *Commentarius super epistolam ad Ebraeos*. Jaena, 1641.

_____: *Loci communes theologici*. Ed. by J. F. Cotta. 21 vols. Tubinga, 1762-87.

GOUGE, W.: *A Learned and Very Useful Commentary on the Whole Epistle to the Hebrews*. 2 vols. London, 1655.

GRAF, J.: *Der Hebräerbrief: wissenschaftlich-praktische Erklärung*. Freiburg i.B., 1918.

GROTIUS, H.: "Annotationes in epistolam ad Hebraeos" in *Opera omnia theologica*. Amstelodamum, 1679. Vol. II, pp. 1010-69.

HAERING, T.: *Der Brief an die Hebräer*. Stuttgart, 1925.

_____: "Gedankengang und Grundgedanken des Hebräerbriefes." *ZNW* 18 (1917-18), 145-64.

HALDANE, J. A.: *An Exposition of the Epistle to the Hebrews*. London, 1860.

HAMMOND, H.: "The Epistle of Paul the Apostle to the Hebrews" in *A Paraphrase and Annotations Upon all the Books of the New Testament*. 4th. ed. London, 1675. Pp. 725-69.

140

_____: *The Miscellaneous Theological Works of Henry Hammond*. Ed. by N. Pocock. Library of Anglo-Catholic Theology. 3 vols. Oxford, 1847-50.

HEINRICHS, J. H.: *Pauli epistola ad Hebraeos graece*. Vol. VIII of J. B. Koppe's *Novum Testamentum*. 2nd. ed. Göttingen, 1823.

HEINSIUS, D.: *Exercitationes sacrae ad Novum Testamentum*. Lugdunum Batavorum, 1639.

HÉRING, J.: *L'Épître aux Hébreux*. Commentaire du Nouveau Testament 12. Paris & Neuchatel, 1955. ET: *The Epistle to the Hebrews*. London, 1970.

HEWITT, T.: *The Epistle to the Hebrews: An Introduction and Commentary*. London, 1960.

HIGGINS, A. J. B.: "Priest and Messiah." *VetT* 3 (1953), 321-36.

_____: "The Priestly Messiah."*NTS* 13 (1967), 211-39.

HOFMANN, J. C. K. von: *Der Schriftbeweis: ein theologischer Versuch*. 2 vols. 2nd. ed. Nördlingen, 1857-60.

_____: "Der Brief an die Hebräer" in *Die Heilige Schrift neuen Testaments zusammenhängend untersucht*. Nördlingen, 1862-78. Vol. V, pp. 53-561.

HOLTZHEUER, O.: *Der Brief an die Hebräer ausgelegt*. Berlin, 1883.

HUNNIUS, G.: *Exegesis epistolae ad Hebraeos, scripta et recognita*. Francofurtum, 1586.

JÉRÔME, F. J.: *Das geschichtliche Melchisedek-Bild und seine Bedeutung im Hebräerbrief*. Freiburg i.B., 1920.

JUSTINIANUS, B.: "In epistolam ad Hebraeos" in *In omnes B. Pauli Apostoli epistolas explanationes*. Lugdunum Batavorum, 1612-13. Vol. II, pp. 601-880.

KÄSEMANN, E.: *Das wandernde Gottesvolk: Eine Untersuchung zum Hebräerbrief*. 4th. ed. Göttingen, 1961.

KEIL, C. F.: *Kommentar über den Brief an die Hebräer*. Leipzig, 1885.

KENNEDY, G. T.: *St. Paulus Conception of the Priesthood of Melchisedech: An Historico-Exegetical Investigation*. The Catholic University of America Studies in Sacred Theology II.63. Washington, D. C., 1951.

KENNEDY, H. A. A.: *The Theology of the Epistles*. London, 1919.

KISTEMAKER, S.: *The Psalm Citations in the Epistle to the Hebrews*. Amsterdam, 1961.

KLEE, H.: *Auslegung des Briefes an die Hebräer*. Mainz, 1833.

KNATCHBULL, N.: *Animadversiones in libros Novi Testamenti*. 3rd. ed. Oxford, 1676.

KUINOEL, C. G.: *Commentarius in epistolam ad Hebraeos*. Leipzig, 1831.

KURTZ, J. H.: *Der Brief an die Hebräer erklärt*. Mitau, 1869.

KUSS, O.: *Der Brief an die Hebräer*. Regensburger Neues Testament 8/1. Regensburg, 1966.

LAPIDE, C. a: "Commentarius in epistolam ad Hebraeos" in
Commentaria in omnes divi Pauli epistolas. Antwerpa, 1734.
Pp. 831-976.

LAUBACH, F.: *Der Brief an die Hebräer*. Wuppertaler Studien-
bibel. Wuppertal, 1967.

LAWSON, G.: *An Exposition of the Epistle to the Hebrews*.
London, 1662.

LE CLERC, J.: "Epistola Pauli Apostoli ad Hebraeos" in *Novum
Testamentum domini nostri Jesu Christi cum paraphrasi et
adnotationibus H. Hammondi*. Amstelodamum, 1698. Vol. II,
pp. 307-48.

_____: *A Supplement to Dr. Hammond's Paraphrase and An-
notations on the New Testament*. London, 1699.

LEONARD, W.: *The Authorship of the Epistle to the Hebrews*.
London, 1939.

LIMBORCH, P.: "Paraphrasis & commentarius in epistolam ad
Hebraeos" in *Commentarius in Acta Apostolorum et in epistolas ad Romanos et ad Hebraeos*. Roterodamum, 1711. Pp.
525-734.

_____: *Theologia christiana*. 4th. ed. Amstelodamum, 1715.

LINDSAY, W.: *Lectures on the Epistle to the Hebrews*. 2 vols.
Edinburgh, 1867.

LÜNEMANN, G.: *Kritisch-exegetisches Handbuch über den Hebräerbrief*. MK 13. 4th. ed. Göttingen, 1878.

LUTHER, M.: "Divi Pauli apostoli ad Hebraeos epistola" in
WA Vol. LVII, pt. 3. ET: "Lectures on Hebrews" in *Luther's
Works*. Ed. by J. Pelikan. Vol. XXVI, pp. 107-241.

_____: *Luthers Vorlesung über den Hebräerbrief 1517/18*.
Anfänge reformatorischer Bibelauslegung 2. Leipzig, 1929.

McCAUL, J. B.: *The Epistle to the Hebrews: A Paraphrastic
Commentary, with Illustrations from Philo, the Targums,
the Mishna and Gemara, etc*. London, 1871.

McLEAN, A.: *A Paraphrase and Commentary on the Epistle to
the Hebrews*. 2nd. ed. London, 1820. Repr. in *The Miscellaneous Works of Archibald McLean*. London, 1847. Vol. I,
pp. 248 ff.

MacNEILL, H. L.: *The Christology of the Epistle to the Hebrews*. Chicago, 1914.

MAIER, A.: *Kommentar über den Brief an die Hebräer*. Freiburg
i.B., 1861.

MANSON, W.: *The Epistle to the Hebrews: An Historical and
Theological Reconsideration*. London, 1951.

MÉDEBIELLE, A.: "Épître aux Hébreux: traduite et commentée"
in *La Sainte Bible* 12. 2nd. ed. Paris, 1938. Pp. 271-372.

MEINERTZ, M.: *Theologie des Neuen Testaments*. Die Heilige
Schrift des Neuen Testaments. 2 vols. Bonn, 1950.

142

MÉNÉGOZ, E.: *La théologie de l'Épître aux Hébreux*. Paris, 1894.

MICHAELIS, J. D.: *Erklärung des Briefes an die Hebräer*. 2nd. ed. Frankfurt & Leipzig, 1780-86.

_____: *Peircii paraphrasis et notae philologicae atque exegeticae in epistolam ad Hebraeos*. Hala, 1747.

_____: *Compendium theologiae dogmaticae*. 2nd. ed. Goettinga, 1784.

_____: *Einleitung in die göttlichen Schriften des Neuen Testaments*. 2 vols. 4th. ed. Göttingen, 1788.

MICHEL, O.: *Der Brief an die Hebräer*. MK 13. 7th. ed. Göttingen, 1936. 12th. ed., 1966.

_____: "Μελχισέδεκ." *TWNT*. Vol. III, pp. 573-75.

MILLIGAN, G.: *The Theology of the Epistle to the Hebrews*. Edinburgh, 1899.

MOFFATT, J.: *A Critical and Exegetical Commentary on the Epistle to the Hebrews*. ICC. Edinburgh, 1924.

_____: *An Introduction to the Literature of the New Testament*. ITL. 3rd. ed. Edinburgh, 1918.

MONTEFIORE, H. W.: *A Commentary on the Epistle to the Hebrews*. London, 1964.

NAGEL, R.: "Über die Bedeutung Melchisedek's im Hebräerbrief." *ThSK* 22 (1849), 332-86.

NAIRNE, A.: *The Epistle of Priesthood*. 2nd. ed. Edinburgh, 1915.

_____: *The Epistle to the Hebrews*. CGTSC. Cambridge, 1917.

_____: *The Alexandrine Gospel*. London, 1917.

NEIL, W.: *The Epistle to the Hebrews*. Torch Commentaries. London, 1955.

NOMOTO, S.: "Herkunft und Struktur der Hohenpriestervorstellung im Hebräerbrief." *NovT* 10 (1968), 10-25.

OUTREIN, J. d': *Der Brief Pauli an die Hebräer*. 4 pts. in 2 vols. Frankfurt & Leipzig, 1713-18.

OWEN, J.: *Exercitations on the Epistle to the Hebrews*. 4 vols. London, 1668-74.

PAULUS, H. E. G.: *Des Apostels Paulus Ermahnungs-Schreiben an die Hebräer-Christen*. Heidelberg, 1833.

_____: *Das Leben Jesu als Grundlage einer reinen Geschichte des Urchristenthums*. 2 vols. Heidelberg, 1828.

PEAKE, A. S.: *The Epistle to the Hebrews*. Century Bible. Edinburgh, 1914.

PEIRCE, J.: *A Paraphrase and Notes on the Epistle to the Hebrews*. London, 1727.

PISCATOR, J.: "Analysis logica epistolae Pauli ad Hebraeos" in *Commentarii in omnes libros Novi Testamenti*. Herborna, 1621. Pp. 1285-1371.

PURDY, A. C. and COTTON, J. H.: "The Epistle to the Hebrews" in *The Interpreter's Bible*. New York & Nashville, 1952-57. Vol. XI, pp. 575-763.

QUENSTEDT, J. A.: *Theologia didactico-polemica sive systema theologicum*. 2 vols. Lipsia, 1715.

RAMBACH, J. J.: *Gründliche und erbauliche Erklärung der Epistel Pauli an die Hebräer*. Frankfurt & Leipzig, 1742.

REUSS, E. W.: "L'Épître aux Hebreux" in *La Bible: Nouveau Testament*. Paris, 1876-78. Vol. V, pp. 9-106.

_____ : *Histoire de la Théologie chrétienne au Siècle apostolique*. 2 vols. 3rd. ed. Strasbourg & Paris, 1864.

RIEHM, E. K. A.: *Der Lehrbegriff des Hebräerbriefes dargestellt*. 2nd. ed. Basel & Ludwigsburg, 1867.

RIGGENBACH, E.: *Der Brief an die Hebräer*. ZK 14. Leipzig, 1913.

ROBINSON, T. H.: *The Epistle to the Hebrews*. Moffatt New Testament Commentary. London, 1933.

ROHR, I.: *Der Hebräerbrief*. Die heilige Schrift des Neuen Testaments 10. 4th. ed. Bonn, 1932.

SCHAEFFER, A.: *Erklärung des Hebräerbriefes*. Die Bücher des Neuen Testaments 5. Münster, 1893.

SCHIERSE, F. J.: *Der Brief an die Hebräer*. Dusseldorf, 1968.

_____ : *Verheissung und Heilsvollendung: Zur theologischen Grundfrage des Hebräerbriefes*. Münchener theologische Studien I.9. München, 1955.

SCHILLE, G.: "Erwägungen zur Hohepriesterlehre des Hebräerbriefes." *ZNW* 46 (1955), 81-109.

_____ : "Die Basis des Hebräerbriefes." *ZNW* 48 (1957), 270-80.

SCHLATTER, A.: "Der Brief an die Hebräer" in *Erläuterungen zum Neuen Testament*. 4th. ed. Stuttgart, 1928 ff. Vol. III, pp. 220-436.

_____ : *Die Theologie der Apostel*. 2nd. ed. Stuttgart, 1922.

SCHLICHTING, J.: "Commentarius in epistolam ad Hebraeos" in *Crellii opera omnia*. Eleutheropolis, 1656. Vol. II, pp. 130 ff.

SCHMIDT, Eras.: "Epistola Pauli ad Hebraeos" in *Notae et animadversiones in Novum Testamentum*. Norimberga, 1658. Pp. 1292-1346.

SCHMIDT, Seb.: *Commentarius in epistolam Pauli ad Hebraeos*. 3rd. ed. Lipsia, 1722.

SCHÖTTGEN, C.: *Horae Hebraicae et Talmudicae*. 2 vols. Dresda & Lipsia, 1733-42.

SCHRÖGER, F.: *Der Verfasser des Hebräerbriefes als Schriftausleger*. Biblische Untersuchungen 4. Regensburg, 1968.

SCHULZ, D.: *Der Brief an die Hebräer; Einleitung, Übersetzung und Anmerkungen*. Breslau, 1818.

SCOTT, E. F.: *The Epistle to the Hebrews: Its Doctrine and Significance*. Edinburgh, 1922.

SEEBERG, A.: *Der Brief an die Hebräer*. Leipzig, 1912.

SEMLER, J. S.: "Beiträge zu genauerer Einsicht des Briefes an die Hebräer in S. J. Baumgarten's *Erklärung des Briefes St. Pauli an die Hebräer*. Halle, 1763. Pp. 3 ff.

SOCINUS, F.: *Socini opera omnia*. 2 vols. Irenopolis, 1656.

SODEN, H. von: "Der Brief an die Hebräer: in *HCNT* III.2. 3rd. ed. Freiburg i.B., 1899. Pp. 1-114.

SOUBIGOU, L.: "Le chapitre VII de l'Épître aux Hébreux." *L'Anneé Théologique* 7 (1946), 69-82.

SOWERS, S. G.: *The Hermeneutics of Philo and Hebrews*. Zürich, 1965.

SPICQ, C.: *L'Épître aux Hébreux*. EBib. 2 vols. Paris, 1952-53.

_____: "L'Épître aux Hébreux, Apollos, Jean-Baptiste, les Hellénistes et Qumran." *RQ* 1 (1958/59), 365-90.

STAPULENSIS, J. F.: *Pauli apostoli epistolae*. Parisius, 1515.

STEIN, K. W.: *Der Brief an die Hebräer theoretisch-practisch erklärt*. Leipzig, 1838.

STENGEL, L.: *Erklärung des Briefes an die Hebräer, nach dem handschriftlichen Nachlass des L. Stengel von J. Beck*. Karlsruhe, 1849.

STEWARD, G.: *The Argument of the Epistle to the Hebrews*. Edinburgh, 1872.

STIER, R. E.: *Der Brief an die Hebräer in 36 Betrachtungen ausgelegt*. 2 vols. 2nd. ed. Brunswick, 1862.

STORK, H.: "Die sogenannten Melchisedekianer." *Forschung zur Geschichte des neutestamentlichen Kanons* VIII.2. Leipzig, 1928. Pp. 2-82.

STORR, G. C.: *Pauli Brief an die Hebräer erläutert*. 2nd. ed. Tübingen, 1809.

STRACK, H. L. and BILLERBECK, P.: *Kommentar zum Neuen Testament aus Talmud und Midrasch*. 4 vols. München, 1922-28.

STRATHMANN, H.: *Der Brief an die Hebräer*. Das Neue Testament Deutsch 9. 8th. ed. Göttingen, 1963.

STUART, M.: *A Commentary on the Epistle to the Hebrews*. London, 1837.

SYKES, A. A.: *A Paraphrase and Notes Upon the Epistle to the Hebrews*. London, 1755.

TAIT, W.: *Meditationes Hebraicae, or a Doctrinal and Practical Exposition of the Epistle of St. Paul to the Hebrews in a Series of Lectures*. 2 vols. London, 1845.

TELLER, W. A.: *Lehrbuch des christlichen Glaubens*. Helmstädt & Halle, 1764.

_____: *Wörterbuch des Neuen Testaments zur Erklärung der christlichen Lehre*. 5th. ed. Berlin, 1792.

THALHOFER, V.: *Das Opfer des alten und des neuen Bundes mit besonderer Rücksicht auf den Hebräerbrief und die katholische Messopferlehre exegetisch und dogmatisch gewürdigt.* Regensburg, 1870.

THEISSEN, G.: *Untersuchungen zum Hebräerbrief.* Studien zum Neuen Testament 2. Gütersloh, 1969.

THOLUCK, F. A. G.: *Kommentar zum Briefe an die Hebräer.* 3rd. ed. Hamburg, 1850.

SAMPSON, F. S.: *A Critical Commentary on the Epistle to the Hebrews.* New York, 1856.

TURNER, S. H.: *The Epistle to the Hebrews in Greek and English.* New York, 1852.

VANHOYE, A.: *La structure littéraire de l'Épître aux Hébreux.* Studia Neotestamentica I. Paris & Bruges, 1963.

VAUGHAN, C. J.: *The Epistle to the Hebrews.* London, 1890.

VOS, G.: *The Teaching of the Epistle to the Hebrews.* Ed. by J. G. Vos. Grand Rapids, 1956.

_____: "The Priesthood of Christ in the Epistle to the Hebrews." *PThR* 5 (1907), 423-447, 579-604.

WEGSCHEIDER, J. A. L.: *Institutiones theologiae christianae dogmaticae.* 4th. ed. Halla, 1824.

WEINEL, H.: *Biblische Theologie des Neuen Testaments: Die Religion Jesu und des Urchristenthums.* 4th. ed. Tübingen, 1928.

WEISS, B.: *Der Brief an die Hebräer.* MK 13. 6th. ed. Göttingen, 1897.

WELCH, A.: *The Authorship of the Epistle to the Hebrews.* Edinburgh & London, 1898.

WESLEY, J.: *Explanatory Notes Upon the New Testament.* London, 1755.

WESTCOTT, B. F.: *The Epistle to the Hebrews.* 2nd. ed. London, 1892.

WETTE, W. M. L. de: "Kurze Erklärung der Briefe an Titus, Timotheus und die Hebräer" in *Kurzgefasstes exegetisches Handbuch zum Neuen Testament.* 2nd. ed. Leipzig, 1838-48. Vol. II, pt. 5, pp. 186 ff.

_____: "Über die symbolisch-typische Lehrart des Briefes an die Hebräer." *Theologische Zeitschrift.* Berlin, 1818-22. Vol. III, pp. 1-57.

WETTSTEIN, J. J.: "Η ΠΡΟΣ ΕΒΡΑΙΟΥΣ ΕΠΙΣΤΟΛΗ" in *Η ΚΑΙΝΗ ΔΙΑΘΗΚΗ.* Amstelodamum, 1751-52. Vol. II, pp. 383-446.

WHITBY, D.: "A Paraphrase With Annotations on the Epistle of St. Paul to the Hebrews" in *A Paraphrase and Commentary on the New Testament.* 7th. ed. London, 1760. Vol. II, pp. 501-83.

WICKHAM, E. C.: *The Epistle to the Hebrews.* The Westminster Commentaries. London, 1910.

WILLIAMSON, R.: *Philo and the Epistle to the Hebrews.* Arbeiten

zur Literatur und Geschichte des hellenistischen Juden-
thums IV. Leiden, 1970.

_____ : *The Epistle to the Hebrews*. Epworth Preacher's
Commentaries. London. 1964.

_____ : "Platonism and Hebrews." *SJT* 16 (1963), 415-24.

_____ : "Hebrews and Doctrine." *ExpT* 81 (1970), 371-76.

WINDISCH, H.: *Der Hebräerbrief*. HNT 14. 2nd. ed. Tübingen,
1931.

WOERNER, E.: *Der Brief St. Pauli an die Hebräer*. Ludwigsburg, 1876.

WOUDE, A. S. van der: "Melchisedek als himmlische Erlösergestalt in den neugefundenen eschatologischen Midraschim aus
Qumran-Höhle XI." *Oudtestamentische Studiën* XIV. Leiden,
1965. Pp. 354-73.

_____ and JONGE, M. de: "11 Q Melchizedek and the New
Testament." *NTS* 12 (1965-66), 301-26.

WUTTKE, G.: *Melchisedech, der Priesterkönig von Salem*. Beihef-
te zur *ZNW* 5. Giessen, 1927.

YADIN, Y.: "The Dead Sea Scrolls and the Epistle to the Hebrews." *Scripta Hierosolymitana* 4 (1958), 36-55.

_____ : "A Note on Melchizedek and Qumran." *IEJ* 15 (1965),
152-54.

ZILL, L.: *Der Brief an die Hebräer übersetzt und erklärt*.
Mainz, 1879.

ZIMMERMANN, H.: *Die Hohepriester-Christologie des Hebräerbriefes*. Paderborn, 1964.

ZWINGLI, U.: "In epistolam beati Pauli ad Hebraeos expositio"
in *Zwingli opera*. Zürich, 1581. Vol. IV, pp. 573 ff.

BEITRÄGE ZUR GESCHICHTE DER BIBLISCHEN HERMENEUTIK

9

Michael Andrew Fahey
Cyprian and the Bible

A Study in Third-Century Exegesis. 1971. V, 696
Seiten. Kart. DM 48.--, Ln. DM 54.--

8

Thomas Willi
Herders Beitrag zum Verstehen des Alten Testaments

1971. VIII, 152 Seiten. Kart. DM 19.--

7

Irmgard Christiansen
*Die Technik der allegorischen Auslegungswissen-
schaft bei Philon von Alexandrien*

1969. V, 191 Seiten. Kart. DM 39.--, Ln. DM 45.--

6

Eberhard Winkler
Exegetische Methoden bei Meister Eckhart

1965. VII, 130 Seiten. Kart. DM 28.--

5

Johann-Friedrich Konrad
Abbild und Ziel der Schöpfung

Untersuchungen zur Exegese von Genesis 1 und 2
in Barths Kirchlicher Dogmatik III, 1. 1962.
X, 273 Seiten. Kart. DM 48.--, Ln. DM 58.--

J.C.B. MOHR (PAUL SIEBECK) TÜBINGEN